'An inspiring and really practical [...] someone who clearly has the experience and experience of working with many wonderful people with dyslexia. This book is for anyone wanting examples of how talent, perseverance and commitment can lead to great success.'
– *Professor Amanda Kirby, Chair in Developmental Disorders at University of South Wales and author of* How to Succeed in Employment with Specific Learning Difficulties

'This book contains fascinating information for people with dyslexia and anyone interested in helping them to achieve. Margaret Malpas makes it clear that high grades at school are not the only route to a fulfilling life, with detail on the significance of determination, rapport, listening skills and creativity. She even explains how procrastination can be useful. There are some truly inspiring nuggets in here to inspire and encourage, plus handy summaries for those not wanting to read it all at once.'
– *Margaret Rooke, author of* Creative, Successful, Dyslexic: 23 High Achievers Share Their Stories

'This is an interesting and insightful book, which has been well-researched and includes relevant case studies to illustrate key traits for the successful dyslexic. My own struggle with undiagnosed dyslexia at school certainly made me more determined and this has played an integral role in my achievements and success.'
– *Alais Winton, author of* The Self-Help Guide for Teens with Dyslexia *and private tutor for young dyslexics*

SELF-FULFILMENT WITH DYSLEXIA

of related interest

Creative, Successful, Dyslexic
23 High Achievers Share Their Stories
Margaret Rooke
Foreword by Mollie King
ISBN 978 1 84905 653 3
eISBN 978 1 78450 163 1

Dyslexia and Mental Health
Helping People Identify Destructive Behaviours
and Find Positive Ways to Cope
Neil Alexander-Passe
Foreword by Michael Ryan and Pennie Aston
ISBN 978 1 84905 582 6
eISBN 978 1 78450 068 9

Dyslexia
How Would I Cope?
Third Edition
Michael Ryden
ISBN 978 1 85302 385 9
eISBN 978 0 85700 055 2

The Self-Help Guide for Teens with Dyslexia
Useful Stuff You May Not Learn at School
Alais Winton
ISBN 978 1 84905 649 6
eISBN 978 1 78450 144 0

SELF-FULFILMENT WITH DYSLEXIA
A BLUEPRINT FOR SUCCESS

MARGARET D. MALPAS MBE

Jessica Kingsley *Publishers*
London and Philadelphia

First published in 2017
by Jessica Kingsley Publishers
73 Collier Street
London N1 9BE, UK
and
400 Market Street, Suite 400
Philadelphia, PA 19106, USA

www.jkp.com

Library of Congress Cataloging in Publication Data
Title: Self-fulfilment with dyslexia : a blueprint for success / Margaret D. Malpas.
Description: London ; Philadelphia : Jessica Kingsley Publishers, 2017. |
   Includes bibliographical references.
Identifiers: LCCN 2016048160 | ISBN 9781785921988 (alk. paper)
Subjects: LCSH: Dyslexia--Popular works. | Dyslexia--Case studies. |
   Self-care, Health--Popular works.
Classification: LCC RC394.W6 M35 2017 | DDC 616.85/53--dc23 LC record available
at https://lccn.loc.gov/2016048160

British Library Cataloguing in Publication Data
A CIP catalogue record for this book is available from the British Library

ISBN 978 1 78592 198 8
eISBN 978 1 78450 472 4

Printed and bound in the United States

Contents

Preface

This is exciting! The research into many successful dyslexic people, and not just the high fliers, is showing us what we all need to do to be successful and self-fulfilled. So this book will give you the keys to successful behaviours and take you through how you can learn the skills that you need. You will also be able to read case study examples of individuals with dyslexia who are already drawing on and optimising their strengths. They are all very able individuals and their story could be yours!

Successful dyslexics in all fields

In all fields, there are incredibly successful people who ascribe much of their success to their dyslexia. We often quote, as examples, Richard Rogers, the architect, or Nigel Kennedy, the violinist, or Jackie Stewart, the racing car driver.

Dyslexic self-made millionaires

Research carried out by the B.B.C. in 2003 on 300 millionaires discovered that 40 per cent of these self-made millionaires were diagnosed with dyslexia and related learning difficulties. Cass Business School has done some research that indicates that 18–30 per cent of entrepreneurs are dyslexic or have related conditions.

Overlap in dyslexia strengths and entrepreneurs

There is also a huge overlap in the competencies of an entrepreneur and dyslexic traits. However, whilst not all successful individuals are millionaires, many others may count their success in other than monetary terms.

'Happiness is not in the mere possession of money; it lies in the joy of achievement, in the thrill of creative effort.'

President Franklin D. Roosevelt

My research on ordinary people who are self-fulfilled

For my research, I looked at ordinary people who were dyslexic or counted themselves as being dyslexic after screening. I have also taken success to be either the ability of the individual to exist at the very least comfortably, or where the individual self-reports that they are or have been successful.

Using dyslexia as an umbrella for all related conditions

This book will give you the keys to successful behaviours and take you through how you can learn the skills that you need. Throughout, I have used the term 'dyslexia', as it is the most common of all the Specific Learning Difficulties (Sp.L.D.s), but these conditions all overlap and often coexist. It is very rare indeed to find someone who is purely dyslexic. Therefore, what is written here is largely applicable to all the other 7 conditions known to be related. If you want to learn more about dyslexia and these related conditions of Dyscalculia, Attention Deficit Hyperactivity Disorder (A.D.H.D.), Attention Deficit Disorder (A.D.D.), Asperger's Syndrome (Autism Level 1), Dyspraxia (D.C.D.), Dysgraphia, and Specific Speech and Language Impairment then there is more information for you in the Notes section, Appendix B.

So, what's stopping us? Let's get going and learn all about what the characteristics of successful dyslexic people are and the research that shows us we can trust this view.

How the book came about

In 2015, I had been voluntarily working with the British Dyslexia Association for almost a decade. I had met thousands of dyslexic individuals during the course of my work. Many of these were super-successful in a particular area, others were quite successful but would have liked to be more effective in some areas, and some were really struggling both economically and with unresolved emotional trauma. I wanted to know what made the difference. There are so many of us with these conditions that it is unlikely that any government will ever really create the opportunities for all to succeed. This started me thinking about whether we could unlock the reasons why some people were successful either despite or because of what their dyslexic condition gave them to work with. So I started to examine the research on adults with dyslexia and other Sp.L.D.s.

Not much research on adults, most on reading
What I found was that there isn't that much research on adults, though there is a huge amount on children with dyslexia. There's also a lot of research on learning to read, write and spell. Even the research on adults is dominated by research on learning to read.

Research is on high fliers and in the U.S.A.
However, I did find some particular studies that were about the factors that made dyslexic adults successful. There was also a high degree of agreement within the results of these research projects on what the factors were. However, these studies were based largely on incredibly high-achieving individuals – these were not your average Joes. I also saw that quite often in other research, the subjects of the research were undergraduates (aged 18–21 years and with good enough school exam passes to enter university). This didn't provide a representative sample of the dyslexic adults

I was meeting either. The research projects I had read about certainly shaped my thinking in this area (and you can read them too as I have included the references to these papers in the Bibliography). The most relevant studies were done in the U.S.A., which meant that the individuals had been schooled in the American system. I was interested in whether the same characteristics would dominate where someone had been schooled in the U.K. or in a system of education based on the U.K. model. I was also left wondering if the things that made the super-heroes successful were the same characteristics that led to success for ordinary dyslexic adults.

Pilot project on ordinary dyslexic adults

In early 2016, I embarked on a pilot research project. In this, I wanted to get the views of dyslexic individuals about what they thought helped them be successful. I also wanted to cover a spread of ages and to include people of economic diversity. Initially, I received answers from 15 adults but this quickly expanded to 32. (The latter 17 individuals, 2 of whom were not dyslexic but were knowledgeable about dyslexia, were attending the B.D.A.'s International Conference and so were either academics or tutors/teachers with a lot of knowledge about dyslexia.) I also asked 5 individuals whom I knew were not dyslexic to complete the questionnaire so that I had a small control group.

My intention when I started this pilot was to use it to re-examine the questions and make sure they worked.

Then I had intended to extend the research and do it on a much bigger sample. However, although there were differences between some of the answers from the 2 groups, generally the results were already very consistent and, as I studied them, I realised that a lot of the characteristics they were describing were things that people could learn. I may well go back to that research later but it seemed like a priority to share this information with adults who were looking for answers as soon as possible.

The questionnaire and the findings are shown in Appendix A. Taking account of the responses from both groups, we can summarise the findings as:

- Determination and grit are essential; empathy is useful.

- Success is due to very hard work and also using your strengths.

- Dyslexia, for most, conveyed strengths especially in seeing the big picture, atypical problem solving and empathy; and those who claimed to have strengths also had higher levels of self-esteem.

- Challenges with dyslexia, or not knowing what it was and how to cope, had limited some individuals' life experiences and results.

- Over half of respondents had someone helping them cope.

- Gaining coping strategies around your individual difficulties is important.

- Disclosure to employers was fairly common, and safer to do in academic or education circles than elsewhere for these respondents.

- Advice to a young person was to get a diagnosis early, become effective at your coping strategies, take confidence – the future will be brighter than you expect, recognise that you are different and celebrate it, adopt a positive mindset.

Whilst not many people were studied in this pilot, I feel we can have confidence in the conclusions about these characteristics that lead to success because of the level of consistency in the findings. We can say with some definiteness that the research shows us that dyslexic adults need to have the following characteristics in order to develop their true potential:

- Strong determination, grit.

- Confidence, self-esteem.

- Passion about their interests.

- Exceptional in the right niche.

- Skilled in atypical problem solving; be good procrastinators.

- Creative.

- Empathetic.

- Good influencers, with great verbal skills.

- Effective, fluent users of good coping strategies.

- It is also important to have strong support from family and mentors.

Supporting evidence

There is also plenty of supporting evidence from outside the field of dyslexia about what makes some people very successful. A recently published book on this is **Grit: The Power of Passion and Perseverance** by Angela Duckworth (May 2016). Her research is also focused on highly achieving individuals. (Interestingly, her post-graduate degree from Oxford University was in studying the neural mechanisms of dyslexia.) Her recent finding is that the most important element in achievement is determination.

Having identified what characteristics are needed for success and self-fulfilment, each chapter in this book takes a deeper look at a particular characteristic. You will be able to read what you need to do to acquire these traits. To read further on the research available on successful dyslexic adults, see the Bibliography at the end of the book.

Chapter 1

You Must Have Determination

'The three great essentials to achieve anything worthwhile are, first, hard work; second, stick-to-itiveness; third, common sense.'

Thomas A. Edison

'The difference between a successful person and others is not a lack of strength, not a lack of knowledge, but rather a lack in will.'

Vince Lombardi Jr

Vincent Lombardi Jr was an American football player, born 11 June 1913 and died 3 September 1970; the N.F.L. Superbowl trophy is named after him. He is considered to be one of the best coaches in N.F.L. history and, while a head coach for N.F.L., he never had a losing season. He was persistent. For me, his quote sums up the importance of determination, sometimes known as having grit. However, I also love Edison's word 'stick-to-itiveness'!

Successful people get there through determination, not just talent

We like to think that extremely successful people have got to where they are because they have an exceptional talent. However, successful individuals, with or without dyslexia, are highly determined, have grit.

You can do the grit scale developed by Professor Angela Duckworth, which you will find at http://angeladuckworth.com.

Struggling with dyslexia as a child may grow determination

'Most people who have made a million have difficult childhoods or have been frustrated in a major way. Dyslexia is one of the driving forces behind that,' said Dr Adrian Atkinson who was a psychologist involved in the B.B.C. research on millionaires. So, the nature of a dyslexic individual's life where they have to struggle from an early age may well incubate this concept of life that they have to be determined to get anywhere.

Determination and hard work are also necessary for dyslexic children learning to be literate. They may have got used to working like this and experienced successes as a result, so their internal programming sets them up to behave like this in future as an adult. Such individuals make very good employees. What employer doesn't want someone who works hard, is really persistent and sociable in a team? This approach can create success at work despite an individual's ongoing challenges with literacy or memory.

Talent is a building block, but skill needs practice

So what is the relationship between raw talent, determination and success? Walt Disney, who was dyslexic, was once sacked from his job at a newspaper, being told he lacked creativity! He was still developing; he needed more practice for his talent to shine through. Talent is a latent ability but it requires practice to turn it into skill. All individuals are born with the potential for strengths as well as weaknesses. There's been a debate for years about whether dyslexia confers some specific strengths, and we don't have a firm answer to this. However, I now argue in this book that we can point to general research on traits such as creativity and problem solving and many dyslexic people do have these traits. We can also identify the characteristics people need, and they can develop their strengths.

As an individual you will know what your talents are, and the key point here is that talent is a building block. It's the start, not the finish, for successful people. When you have developed a lot of skill, your perception for the task and its context changes. You can see this from the way in which professional sport is now run. There is a role in football, rugby, baseball and all professional sports now to gather statistics. So, we have talented sportsmen and women, who have practised for years. Then we have the statisticians and coaches who take apart the games that have been played and draw certain conclusions on micro-managing set pieces within the play. This is beyond talent and beyond skill – it is interpreting events at an expert level and realising how to improve still further. This is exactly what people who are extremely successful do. They have talent, they practise to develop skill and they continue to reflect throughout their lives on how they can be even better at what they do.

Success comes from learning from failure

In fact, we know that success comes about through a cycle of experiences, including failures, that you learn from and eventually you get to success. This requires determination.

Steve Jobs, also dyslexic, found success in his 20s with Apple, but when he was in his 30s the Apple board of directors dismissed him. Jobs then founded a new company, NeXT, which was eventually acquired by Apple and then Jobs took Apple to even more success. He was demonstrating determination.

Idea of continuous improvement

Many management processes, such as self-development, quality assurance models and Total Quality Management, are all based on this idea of continuous improvement, making small incremental steps that involve working out what will work (and inevitably what doesn't, i.e. failures) and then becoming more successful, which requires grit and determination. So, we need to acquire the determination to keep going in the face of failure and to learn from it.

Can we learn from unsuccessful dyslexics?

It is worth at this point considering briefly the opposite of what we are investigating. What about the dyslexic adults who do not consider themselves to be successful, or who we would generally feel do not have happy, fulfilled lives? Is there something we can learn from them?

Lack of literacy results in no or low-level jobs

First, it is necessary to be able to handle written materials in order to be able to study or work effectively. Traditionally, it was thought that dyslexic individuals would go into manual jobs because they wouldn't be able to do jobs involving literacy. Of course, that now presents a significant problem as we have far fewer manual jobs. Those that do exist still require some literacy – for reading safety rules and often recording outcomes, for example. This situation will get worse in the future when the likelihood will be that there will be fewer jobs, and those that exist will require higher levels of skill. However, I digress somewhat. The key point is that it is very difficult to be economically successful if you cannot read or write at all. So those children who do not learn to read and write, or have alternative coping strategies such as fluently using technology, are at a huge disadvantage in adulthood.

Growing up not believing you can achieve leads to low self-esteem

Our experience as children sets up patterns of thinking and behaviour as adults. If you can't do things your peers can do, if your hard work and determination doesn't result in a good outcome, then a spiral of negative thinking patterns can begin. This is aggravated by a lack of diagnosis – often people do not know that their challenges exist as a result of dyslexia. Without diagnosis, or at least a glimmer that this may be the root cause of problems with learning to be literate, there may be no effective learning processes set up. As a result, instead of believing you can do anything you set your heart on, you may grow up believing that you cannot do anything. Even worse, you may believe that it's always your fault when things go wrong. This results in, at best, unstable self-esteem and we will see in Chapter 2 how crucial self-esteem is for success.

Self-knowledge and positive mindset leads to a virtuous cycle

The result for many with low literacy is a poor understanding of themselves, consequential low self-esteem and negative thinking patterns. This can result in serious stress from being unable to pay bills and frustration at being unemployed. For those who are functionally illiterate, the result now, when we depend so much on digital communications, is isolation from mainstream society. As adults, if they get a job, they may well be forced to lie about their difficulties rather than create positive strategies, and this makes them feel worse about themselves. So what we have is a very vicious cycle. This does teach us that what we need to create for self-fulfilment is a virtuous cycle.

This is exactly what the respondents in the research meant when advising a young person. They advocated getting a diagnosis of dyslexia early so that you have time to come to terms with what it means for you. Recognise that you have strengths and things that you are good at and use these to grow and maintain good self-esteem. Learn or work out effective coping strategies for things you find more challenging. Interestingly, the second group of respondents spoke about creating a positive mindset, which wasn't suggested by the questions but was consistently brought up. This was clearly something those respondents who had been successful in education had recognised as important to their successes. A significant part of a positive attitude is learning to reflect appropriately on experiences.

How we learn successfully

Let's look at how we learn to learn effectively. Everything we learn from experience is based on reflecting on how things could have been done better. Whenever we do anything important, we should reflect to see if there are lessons to learn and improvements to make next time. Figure 1.1 demonstrates this.

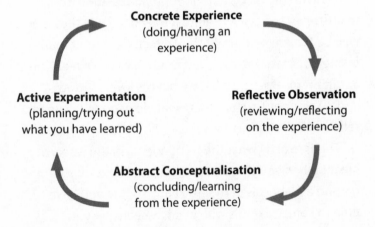

Figure 1.1 Kolb's learning cycle

This is Kolb's learning cycle, which he produced in 1984. The idea is that every time we experience anything, we can maximise what we can learn from it. We need to first reflect upon the experience, then draw any general conclusions from it (conceptualise) and finally modify our behaviour according to what we have discovered. This is the very epitome of continuous improvement and learning that leads eventually to a successful outcome. So, now you can try this out.

Exercise in learning well

Think of something you did recently. It really can be anything, but preferably something that you wanted to go well. Now, examine it against the headings in the learning cycle model.

So, you have had an experience, now you are thinking about it (reflecting), what went well, what didn't go so well? Have you learned something to apply more generally from this (conceptualising)? What would you do differently next time (modifying)?

Learn to reflect

Successful individuals are reflective. They make this cycle of continuously improving their skills and behaviour into part of everyday life. They learn to do it automatically. You may know that it is also a significant part of most training courses and that, in the professions, it is used to underpin all continuous professional development (C.P.D.) requirements for post-qualification development. In fact, it is seen to be so important that most professional bodies, such as A.C.C.A. for accountants, C.I.P.D. for Personnel Managers and the B.D.A. for specialist teachers, make a mandatory element of C.P.D. a requirement for continued membership of their professional body.

Dyslexics learn differently

One of the things you may often hear is that 'dyslexics are not disabled, they just learn differently'. It is definitely true that many dyslexics do learn differently but actually, in my experience, everyone has a learning preference. So what are these differences? They have generally come about because of the things that we can do, rather than those we find difficult. Therefore, we learn better if we can use our global understanding, big picture skills, to first get an understanding of the overview of the topic to be learned. We need to learn using all our senses, as some may be a bit weaker than others. This means seeing, hearing and feeling things (in fact, everyone learns better this way whether they are dyslexic or not). We may prefer to move while learning rather than just sit, and we may like being part of a group so that learning is based on discussion. The key point to all of this is that to be a successful learner, we need to understand our personal preferences and be confident to ensure that we access learning in this way.

How to learn from your failures

We often bask in our successes, but failures are even more important to learning and our personal development. Professor Rob Kaplan of Harvard Business School encourages his students to reflect on their success story and their failure story. Your failures are defining. They explain how you operate; they expose your quirks, insecurities and blind spots. The only way to improve as a manager, leader or entrepreneur is to reflect on failures to learn from them.

Richard Branson's determination

Why didn't Richard Branson give up after his first failure? Richard found school to be something of a nightmare for him; he is dyslexic. He enjoyed sport, though, and was captain of the football, rugby and cricket teams. By the time he was 15, he had already developed 2 ventures – growing Christmas trees and raising budgerigars. Both the ventures eventually failed but he probably learned a lot from the experiences and, as we know, has gone on to an illustrious entrepreneurial career. The answer to why he didn't give up is that he has determination.

Keeping motivated is an important factor in being determined

Something was motivating Branson to keep going. If you have a passion, then it can be quite easy to remain motivated; in fact, at times, it could become an obsession. The healthy version of determination and motivation is called 'harmonious determination'. This means that whilst you are interested enough to keep going, you can still have a life outside your passion. It doesn't entirely define you so if, for any reason, it subsequently failed, you would be able to pick yourself up and do something else.

However, sometimes, particularly when things are not going so well, and success is not coming as easily as we hoped, we are not so motivated. We need to motivate ourselves and here is how we do that.

How to keep yourself motivated

Everyone has drives, and motivation is the motive power to enable us to satisfy a drive. Some drives are physical, such as to satisfy thirst, hunger, safety or the need for sex; others are more abstract, such as the desire for self-development or to be loved or accepted. These drives will motivate our behaviour, for example if we are thirsty to get a drink and so on.

Having drive

We need to be motivated to act in the first place. In our research, the respondents recommended to young people that they thought about their talents and believed in themselves. What talents do you have; could these be the sources of your motivation? Sometimes, though, if our motivation is flagging we need to think of a way to maintain our motivation. Usually, what maintains our motivation is getting successes. Consequently, when what we actually get is failures, then that can act as a demotivator. What distinguishes really successful people is that they keep going – they have intrinsic motivation, or drive.

People who believe in you can help

We cannot underestimate the role that others can play in increasing and maintaining our determination. Perhaps we should say that 'behind every successful dyslexic person is a partner, friend or mentor who is rooting for them'! The individuals who support dyslexic people give them confidence, pick them up when they are down and encourage them when they are about to give up. We can certainly see this from the research, where many of the individuals said that their success was in part due to a sympathetic teacher seeing beyond their difficulties or a partner that believed in them. This is where parents and mentors play an essential role, and you can read more about that later, in Chapter 10.

Things you value and are passionate about can motivate you

Successful people with dyslexia often succeed because they are passionate about something and that motivates them intrinsically. Another point about passion is that usually it's related to something you deeply care about. A psychologist, Victor Vroom, wrote that people undertake things because they value the end reward. If they continue to value the end reward, they will keep going. However, if they stop valuing the end reward, then their motivation will go down (usually quite quickly). So we can see that if we want to be a success at something it's a good idea to choose something we are passionate about and really value. That way we won't find being determined and having grit too difficult. Here's an interesting story to illustrate that point.

Story about passion and determination

A key person in the founding of the British Dyslexia Association was Marion Welchman. Marion was Welsh, a nurse and probably our first recorded 'Tiger Mum'. On learning that her son, Howard, was having difficulty learning to be literate, she set about seeing what she could do about this. Her research led to contacts with supportive medics and 11 others with whom she set up the first local association, the Bath Association for Dyslexia (B.A.S.D.), in 1972. Marion acted as secretary of the Association.

Her priority was to ensure that teachers gained the knowledge of the Orton and Gillingham teaching methods, and by dint of jumble sales and the like, the funding was found for the first 4 courses. She spoke at many meetings as dyslexia awareness grew, and quickly more local associations were setting up. This led to lots of phone calls to Marion for help and information.

Marion directed a very successful assessment and teaching centre, which eventually became the Dyslexia Institute. Focus quickly turned to influencing government and an umbrella organisation for the local associations was required, and Marion was one of those responsible for founding the B.D.A. She became, through her contacts, a remarkable ambassador and persuaded international talents to present at a series of conferences from 1970. So we have this tiger mum of astonishing talents to thank not only for the B.D.A., but also for her work in the founding of Dyslexia Action.

Marion was extremely passionate about dyslexia, about children like her son getting appropriate help. This passion gave her the motivation to be very determined and her campaigning and sheer hard work eventually paid off with recognition by the government and others that dyslexia does exist.

How determined are you compared with others?

Here are some questions to help you go about building your determination:

- How do you compare with your friends' levels of determination? Ask those you trust to see if you can get a crude benchmark of how determined you naturally are.

- Is there something that you've always dreamed of tackling? Is there something that you really value and are passionate about? Could this thing lead to success for you?

- Are you naturally intrinsically motivated (you are just motivated by something inside you) or are you dependent on praise or rewards to be motivated?

- What are your strengths? Do you have a real talent for something (it doesn't matter what this is)?

From the answers to these questions, you should be able to identify what you would be prepared to be sufficiently determined about. These are really deep questions and you may find that you need to take time to reflect on them. You may find that you need to return to the questions over time. Finally, you may find that you just haven't met your real passion yet, and that's O.K. too.

SELF-FULFILMENT WITH DYSLEXIA

What does success mean for you?

At this point, we really need to return to the idea
of what success means for you. Are you looking for
commercial success, or success in the arts, sport or
science? Or perhaps you are concerned with society
and the environment and want to achieve something
there. All of these things have different contexts and so
it will be important to think about how to go about the
thing you want to do, taking into account the context it
exists in. We can return to this point when we talk about
decision making.

Case study: Kenny Logan

Kenny Logan is an entrepreneur and retired international
rugby player. He made his debut for Scotland in
1992 against Australia, won 70 caps and retired from
international rugby union in 2003. He founded Logan
Sports Marketing in 1999, a successful sponsorship and
events consultancy, and is a director of Klas International
which is a networking business.

Kenny, a farmer's son, says he didn't enjoy school.
He was off for days and weeks with stomach aches and
anxiety. Teachers described him as stupid and labelled
him as thick, whilst he was trying hard every day but
not succeeding in academic subjects. However, he was
the fastest child in the school and found some respite
in P.E. and games. Deirdre Wilson, a teacher who took
the remedial class, thought Kenny might be dyslexic,

and at the time Kenny thought he could take a course of antibiotics and be better within 10 days! Of course, this was not to be and Kenny describes school as 'a punishment'. Deidre's prognosis might well have been correct but nothing was done at school to help Kenny. At age 15, Kenny was in the school hall about to sit public exams. After ten minutes, he got up and left, with just his name written on his paper. The invigilating teacher asked him where he was going. His response was, 'You know I can't read or write so what's the point of me staying.' He kept walking and never looked back.

However, his sports teacher saw potential in young Kenny and coached him hard. Kenny was also going to the local rugby club, Stirling County, with his cousins. He was good at all sports but liked rugby best and it was the sport he showed the most flair for. So Kenny worked on the farm and trained in rugby. Eventually he was spotted by national coaches for the age groups.

When Kenny was 20, his father died so he took over running the farm to help his mother. This was fine as there wasn't much need to read and write in that job. However, his outstanding skills as a rugby player were soon noticed, and Kenny was capped for Scotland in 1992. In 1995, the sport turned professional and this led to huge opportunities and changes for men like Kenny. He moved to play for Wasps in England, and won 3 Premiership titles and one European Cup along with countless other trophies and honours. He played in 3 Rugby World Cups (R.W.C.) and retired from international rugby in 2003 after the Australian R.W.C.

Moving to London created many issues for Kenny with his lack of literacy. However, he got around this by various means, including subletting to flatmates for no rent in exchange for them paying the utility bills and doing any form-filling. None of his friends knew he was dyslexic at this time. Then he met Gabby, his future wife. She was the first to challenge him over his reading and writing. She had spotted his subterfuges but when he admitted he couldn't read, his first concern was whether she would finish the relationship with him because of his dyslexia. She countered with: 'You're a very clever man but you just don't realise it.' He embarked on a physical literacy programme. Eventually his reading and writing skills improved, as did his focus and processing, so much so that his coach Ian McGeechan asked him if he was taking drugs because his accuracy on the pitch was so much better than before.

Fifteen years on, Kenny says that he's now thriving and feels good about himself. He should, as he has also shown entrepreneurial skills with his business interests. He says that he was always looking at opportunities to make money, even as a child. He puts down his successes to a determination to prove others wrong; he says this determination is in his D.N.A.: 'Even if I couldn't do it, I always put my hand up, I always tried my hardest.' He's still doing this in business, where he says clients know that 'we will deliver' and if he succeeds at something, then he simply moves the bar up for his next challenge.

Key points from this chapter

★ It is crucially important for success that you are determined and can continue working on something potentially for years rather than months.

★ Talent is important but it's only the starting point.

★ You need to be motivated to do anything, and determination requires motivation.

★ It's easier to be motivated when you are doing something you are passionate about and value.

★ The pathway to success is littered with failures.

★ Failures point out our individual ways of operating, and analysing them gives us the best clues for how we work.

★ Successful individuals learn from their mistakes or failures by reflecting upon them, drawing generalisations from them and then modifying what they do in future.

Chapter 2

You Must Have Self-esteem

'The best way to not feel hopeless is to get up and do something. Don't wait for good things to happen to you. If you go out and make some good things happen, you will fill the world with hope.'

Barack Obama

What is self-esteem?

Successful individuals with dyslexia are confident; they have gained high self-esteem. So what is self-esteem? It is about feeling we can cope and that others recognise this in us. What we need to achieve is to be in a virtuous cycle where our self-esteem is constantly reinforced.

Low self-esteem is common in dyslexic children

Unfortunately, low self-esteem is very prevalent in children with dyslexia. We all recognise this pattern of knowing we are good at some things, but not being very good at the things at school that we are initially taught and measured upon. Whoopi Goldberg is dyslexic and the other children called her 'dumb' at school. Fortunately, her mother told her not to listen to them and that she could be anything she wanted to be. Goldberg says she listened to this advice and the rest, as they say, is history.

Give children lots of experiences to mitigate difficulties

When children go to school and are trying but not succeeding to learn to read, spell, write, do arithmetic, organise their P.E. kit, and have the right books with them for lessons, things they see their peers achieving without too much effort, it is very damaging to their self-esteem. They can easily enter a vicious cycle of believing they are not good at anything. The late Professor Bob Burden did research on this area and found that as early as 8 years of age, children decided whether they were going to be learners or not. Parents have a challenge with this, but by giving children lots of opportunities to try out many things and hopefully find something they enjoy, are good at and – even better – become passionate about, then they can mitigate the effects and maintain their children's self-esteem.

Low self-esteem can mean you focus only on risks

The problem with self-esteem is that without it, no one can learn as they are too busy mitigating potential risk and damage to themselves. It's quite scary to feel that you are not going to be able to cope in any situation, and that is what it is like if your self-confidence is really low. So, whilst all individuals need confidence to succeed, this can be a particular challenge for some dyslexic adults.

Nevertheless, it is always possible to raise someone's self-esteem, so now we will learn how you can increase yours. Since self-esteem is about feeling able to cope and be a valuable member of society, it is easy to see that experiencing success, or sometimes just needing to recognise one's own successes, is the way forward.

How to raise your self-esteem

There are 5 ways to build self-esteem, as described below.

Success builds further success

Success is critical in building and reinforcing an individual's self-esteem (just as failure can be very bad for knocking self-esteem unless you really can learn to see failure as on the journey to success, as referred to earlier). So the first way is to build it through experiencing success. A good idea is to pick something quite easy to achieve and then, as confidence grows, more challenging things can be taken on. If you wanted to be a really successful mountain climber, you would probably tackle a hill before attempting to climb Everest! As challenges get harder you will find that you need more motivation to succeed, so we are back to requiring determination and grit again for that.

Reduce risks, increase resilience

Our self-confidence cannot increase if we feel we are at risk. Therefore, the second way to build esteem is to satisfy our need for security. Again, the way to do this is to tackle things that feel only slightly scary to begin with, and build up your resilience to risk by taking on more difficult challenges later. There are things you can do to reduce risk too. So, to take the mountain climbing example again, if you know that you have a good team around you, that your equipment has been thoroughly tested and that the weather report suggests good weather, then all these things reduce the potential risks. This example of risk reduction is applicable in all situations.

Allied to this idea are some interesting conversations circulating about how we should bring up our children. We are much more risk-averse for our children than people were 100 years ago. As a consequence, there is considerable evidence that our children are growing up with less resilience because they are not getting practice at coping with small risks, being on their own and experimenting.

Be better than your peers

The third way to increase your self-esteem doesn't show the human race in particularly good terms! Think about how you feel when you win or you get a better score or result at something than someone else. You may feel slightly superior or happier. Perhaps this happens if your preferred sports team wins over the competition. So self-esteem increases when we compare ourselves with our peers – if we are doing as well or even slightly better. The reason behind this is that self-esteem is about being comfortable in your own skin and feeling competent so that you feel valuable and capable, not ignored or useless. The way we do this is to measure ourselves against others, and so we feel more confident if we feel we are doing better than our neighbours.

Build your capabilities

Fourth, we need to be able to build our capabilities. Our self-esteem will grow if we have the chance to resolve problems and, through this, realise that we are capable. In fact, many adults with dyslexia are particularly good at problem solving and this is an area that is rich with opportunities to develop our confidence further.

Exercise

Finally, the feel-good chemicals that are released when we undertake physical activities, serotonin and encephalin, are really good for increasing feelings of self-esteem, even if only for the short term. Another good reason for getting off the sofa!

Use self-approval

There are a few things you can do immediately that will help you build your self-esteem further. We all have things we are good at or that other people value in us. Think about 3 of these things and repeat them to yourself twice a day. This will train your brain to believe that you are capable and valuable. Interestingly, research done at the University of Colorado found that when offenders gave themselves this kind of affirmation, their test results were improved without any other intervention.

Recognise your successes

Sometimes, we are not good at giving ourselves a pat on the back for our successes. This can be humility, but also if someone's self-esteem is really low then they simply do not believe that they can be the author of success. So, there is a really important technique for recognising your own success and attributing it correctly. Here is how that works.

Recognising your success

Take a look at 3 things you have been involved in which have led to success. Can you identify the part you played in the success? It could be that you were the sole agent and so all the success was down to you. Great, you can take the credit and, most importantly, feel good about yourself and see that you are very capable, so self-esteem rises.

Recognising your part in team success

What about something where you were part of a team that achieved success. What part did you play? Can you see what you did and, therefore, claim the success for that bit? This is still a success story but in this situation it is not uncommon, especially with individuals who are dyslexic, to not take the accolade. It is possible that some of this is due to the individual learning to keep a low profile at school or college, to hide in case they are at risk. These are not behaviours that encourage growth in self-esteem. So we need to be able to measure our own contribution and take the credit for it, even if it's only to ourselves.

The worst scenario is where the individual doesn't recognise the successes they have but counts themselves responsible for all the contributions in failures! This is not uncommon if the person has very low self-esteem, which may have come about through bullying (and I would include in that being told you are 'stupid' or 'thick' at school when you have dyslexia and could easily be helped).

Recognising partial success

So here is how to learn to deal with partial attribution for success or failure. Reflect on the experience, be it a success or a failure, and ask yourself the following questions:

- Was the experience a total success, partial success, partial failure or total failure?

- How much of the experience were you responsible for? Can you put a crude percentage estimate on this?

- How much control did you have over what was done, and how? Again, can you put a crude percentage estimate on this?

From these points you can work out to what extent you were responsible for its success or failure. You can also work out whether any of it is down to you, because if you don't have control over the experience then it is neither your responsibility nor is the result down to you. Let's take an example so you can see this in practice.

Example exercise

Imagine you are working as part of a team to create a cloud catcher. Yes, I know that's ridiculous but it's time for some light relief! Who decided that the team was going to work on a cloud catcher? What and how much of a contribution did you make within the team? Was the objective, or the resources you had at your disposal, within your control? This project was going to fail from the outset as the objective is impossible. If you were also only given a fishing net to catch the clouds then the resources were insufficient and that would contribute to failure too. I would imagine by now you are getting the idea of success attribution.

Case study: Pamela Uddin

Pamela was born in Germany to her Irish mother and Pakistani father. As a child she grew up listening to 3 languages, English, German and Urdu. As a result, she can speak English and German and can understand Urdu. When she was aged 4 they relocated to Ireland. She went to a small primary school in southern Ireland. School was difficult. By age 6, she had already told her mum that the letters on the blackboard wobbled and had been to an optician who prescribed glasses. In her later primary years, her teachers wanted to hold her back a year as she was a distracted, fidgety child. She also had a bad speech impediment and became quiet and introverted. She was bullied as the teachers had described her as 'the stupid girl in the class' and had low self-esteem. Pamela's mum spent up to 5 hours each evening working with her on her homework, and spelling tests on Fridays always resulted in tears. The teachers felt that Pamela wasn't bright and refused to put her forward for a funded assessment in dyslexia. Mum, by this stage a single parent bringing up Pamela alone, saved up for some time and then paid for a private dyslexia assessment when Pamela was 12.

She went to secondary school without having the skills to study. However, there she did have some help from a support teacher, but it wasn't sufficient. Software was provided but Pamela's stammer made it impossible for her to use voice-to-text software. Her final school exams loomed and she couldn't read and comprehend sufficiently or write the answer to the question fast enough. She was good at maths as long as she could understand what it referred to. In English, you had to write an essay where you were only given a title. So, Mum stepped in again and wrote essays which Pamela then learned by heart. She could then just adapt the introduction and the ending, but if she stumbled on the content, she was adrift. She decided to go to college after school to study for a 4-year degree in marketing. She got a scholarship to go to college for those in difficult economic circumstances. She achieved this through an interview and was the first person in her family to do a degree course.

Pamela really struggled in her first year and wanted to give up, but Mum kept her going. She got a tutor and this signalled a big change. Her tutor showed her how to use coping strategies and also described how her brain worked. She also told her that she would have to do extra work but it would be worth it in the long term. She said, 'If you don't change, nothing changes, you'll get the same outcomes.' Pamela took notes in lectures, then at home wrote the notes up and colour-coded them. 'I had to understand myself, first my challenges and then my strengths. I had to change how I approached everything.'

By year 2, Pamela had gained sufficient confidence to be her own advocate. She talked to the lecturers about what she needed and found they were very helpful. She then started to see the strengths she had, that others didn't. She had many more creative ideas than her peers. At the end of year 2, her results were in the top 5 per cent and she got the Dean's award. She achieved similar results in years 3 and 4. Her final dissertation demonstrated her particular creative thinking skills. The topic was 'Corporate culture and the development of the Irish Government'. She analysed this within the context of the contemporary financial crisis, not something anyone else had done. She won a national award for this thesis and met the marketing directors of Coca Cola and Topaz. She graduated with a first class honours degree in marketing. She had never expected that she would be able to achieve something like this and whilst it had been very hard work, she was very proud of her success. 'The education system wasn't built for my brain's operation and I had to change and adapt.'

Topaz's Director had offered to mentor her and he asked her what she wanted to do next. 'I want to go to the University College of Dublin to do a Masters degree. It's in the top 50 business schools in the world.' Realistically, she couldn't afford the high fees. However, a friend of hers heard of a scholarship on the radio and so Pamela applied and was invited to a panel interview. Afterwards, she heard that she had got 1 of only 13 global scholarships to do an M.Sc. in International Business. It wasn't an easy road, though. There was little support for learning there and she was away from home for the first time. She felt isolated as the other students came from extremely affluent backgrounds. She had to learn new skills about mixing with people, and life skills, but these have been very useful since. Some topics were very hard. For example, finance was about hedge funds and this was totally new to her. 'You can't be afraid and stay in your box, you have to be willing to change.' Pamela did change: she developed a love of learning. She challenged herself and found that when you learn something new, it gives you a real buzz. This resulted in a first class M.Sc.

Pamela applied and got a job with L'Oréal in Dublin. She had thought that would be the end of studying but actually the pace picked up and she found she only had weeks to learn new things. She realised that she would have to find new ways to work as the company were not going to change their processes and so she had to be the one to adapt. There were many late nights spent figuring out new coping strategies.

A reality programme, billed as entrepreneur's development, was popular on U.K. T.V. and also appeared in the U.S.A. Pamela decided to give it a go and so appeared on 'The Apprentice'. Whilst it was tough, it was also a profound learning development experience for her. When the programme was airing, she heard from lots of people with dyslexia and with stammers. They often had low confidence and it taught her that there was nothing wrong with her, she could be special. She then applied to work for Unilever and found another useful lesson there. 'I found a group of friends there and they were really helpful to me. I have realised that it really helps me to have colleagues that I can work with.' Her advice to others is to find friends and be open with them about yourself and your challenges as they can help you.

Pamela is now working with a small organisation in a consulting role. She helps them adapt the processes and procedures that large organisations deploy.

Having found these difficult to adjust to, there is a certain irony in her helping other organisations to make these same processes work for them. If you met her, you would never guess that she had a severe stammer either, as that is another thing Pamela has worked at in a determined way.

'I couldn't have done any of this without the support of my mum. She was my rock, always there for me and keeping me determined.'

Key points from this chapter

★ Self-esteem is essential for achieving anything.

★ Self-esteem is about seeing yourself as a competent individual who is valuable to others and society.

★ It is quite common for self-esteem to be lower in individuals with dyslexia than others because they have experienced failures early in life which sets them apart from their peers.

★ You can build self-esteem in small and incremental steps.

★ There are 5 ways to build self-esteem:
  • Achieving successes.
  • Reducing any feelings of risk.
  • Recognising that you are as good or better than your peers at some things.

- Building up your capabilities.

- Doing physical exercise.

★ It is important to recognise your part in a successful or failed outcome. Some things are out of our control.

Chapter 3

You Must Have Passion

*'Far and away the best prize that life offers is the chance
to work hard at work worth doing.'*

Theodore Roosevelt

Importance of passionate interests

The characteristic that successful people have and we
are talking about next is having a passionate interest.
You really only have to look at the following examples
of famous dyslexic people to see that they are, or were,
all passionate about their topic:

Steven Spielberg (Film director)

Magic Johnson (Basketball player)

Erna Solberg (Norwegian Prime Minister)

Carol Greider (Nobel Prize winning microbiologist)

Philip Schultz (Pulitzer prize winning poet)

Jennifer Aniston (Actor)

Peter Leitch (New Zealand businessman and philanthropist)

Richard Rogers (Architect)

Lee Kuan Yew (First Prime Minister of Singapore)

John Chambers (C.E.O. of Cisco)

Steve Fielding (Australian politician)

…and many more.

Research and experience show us that many dyslexic individuals learn to read when they get absorbed in a particular interest. It is their passion that enables them to be determined. They were not good readers but they had to read to find out more about the thing they were interested in. (It's a bit easier now as we have the opportunity to use assistive technology and have print read to us.) However, if you stick at reading, you gain the practice that is often required to master this skill, or at least get good enough at it. This is shown in the case study in Chapter 5 on Geoff Blackwell, who learned to read when his parents took him on a long trip away from other forms of entertainment.

Losing passion in life

Sometimes the daily grind drives the passion out of our lives – we simply don't have time for it. Often we pick jobs not because they really interest us but because they will pay our bills. For whatever reason, it may be necessary to think about reconnecting with what makes you passionate. Your passion is what brings you joy in life.

Refreshing passions

You need to become curious again. Think about your childhood – what did you love to do? Make a list of all the things you engaged in as hobbies as a child. What about the projects, activities or visits you did as a young person – do these suggest things you could reconnect with? Would you enjoy some of these activities now or could they be developed from a childhood hobby to something adults do and, even better, can create wealth from?

Getting started

When people want to do interior design, they often create a 'mood board'. Can you do that with things that interest you? As you begin to think along these lines, you may be surprised at what pops out of your thoughts. If it's a business idea, you can start with a business plan and insert your aim, then break it down into steps that could help you achieve the aim, and so on into plans to cover costs, prices, resources needed, marketing and construction plans. When you experience gaps in your plans, you will be able to think about or seek solutions and that will take you further along your reflection.

Stimulus from famous dyslexics

We have already talked about famous dyslexic people, but can they give you ideas about what you might be passionate about? Or are there other people that you admire? What do you admire about them? Can the individuals in the case studies in this book give you inspiration?

What skills do you have, and why?

These ideas all come from looking outside yourself, but you could look inside too. What are you good at, what skills do you possess? There must have been a reason for you to put in the effort to develop your skills, so does that give you a clue about where your passion lies?

Passion from values

Very often our passions either relate to things that interest us, such as music or sport or intellectual pursuits; or they relate to morality and things we value. These may include things such as fairness, empathy with those in need, or animal welfare; or could involve both interests and values, such as valuing the arts. It is useful to examine what your values are and you may uncover your passions that way.

What sort of success do you seek?

So far, we have considered finding your passions as a way of maintaining motivation and determination alone. Now we need to think about what sort of success you seek. Is it to have a happy life, close relationships with others, to be the best you can at something, or to go after work that you can be passionate about? If you are looking for a hobby to enrich your life, that's fairly straightforward and generally low risk.

When will I know I have found my passion?

You may ask, how will I know that I have found my passion? Well, remember that passion is what brings you joy. You may find that you feel more alive when you are doing something or you become totally immersed, in the flow, and you don't even notice time passing. If you find something you enjoy one day, then do it again the next, and if you still find it's absorbing your interest then you may be onto something. At this stage don't worry about failures, just think about the process. Are you enjoying yourself, are you learning new things, do you yearn to have another go?

Flagging interest

If you find something initially interesting but your interest flags, then don't worry about it, try another activity. The only thing to look out for is that if you are learning new things and then you reach a plateau, that can be a bit frustrating and your enthusiasm may flag. If so, leave it for a week or 2 and go back to it. Your brain may have resolved whatever you found a bit difficult and you will start learning again. If not, then it's not the passion you are seeking and that's O.K.

Sometimes, there are factors in our lives that limit our experimentation. We may not have much time, we may be too tired or we may have limiting thoughts. This is why we need to try things out. It might be just for a short pocket of time, but if you do things that interest you then you will become more energised and that's a reward in itself.

Do you seek the dream of self-employment?

However, some people seek the dream, to turn their passions into self-employment and seek success – and that is rather a different proposition. Running your own business is a bit like being on a treadmill at high speed. It's exhilarating and you may make your fortune. It's certainly a journey like no other. From studying successful dyslexic people, it is apparent that many of them have an overlap of aptitudes with the competencies of entrepreneurs. We also have that interesting statistic that 1 in 6 self-made millionaires in the U.K. are dyslexic. So now let's turn our attention to that.

Caution

Just a word of caution first, though. There are lots of failed businesses that people have started because they liked doing something but didn't take into account that there might not be a market for their products. So if you are thinking along these lines, the first questions to ask yourself are:

- Is there a market for this product or service?

- Will people have the money to pay for it and will they be willing to pay?

Your risk profile

The other important thing to think about if you are considering self-employment is that people have different risk profiles. Some people are entirely comfortable about just going for it, but others will be constantly worried. The latter is counter-productive to self-confidence, which is not helpful. So, you may want to dip your toe in the water and start with a small commercial venture before you put all your time and resources into something.

Characteristics of entrepreneurs and dyslexics

So, you have been warned. But let's now look at this overlap between entrepreneurial aptitudes and the characteristics of successful dyslexic adults.

Entrepreneurs need to be...	Successful dyslexic adults are...
Able to read the landscape to spot opportunities	Able to read the context/ market
Persistent and determined	Persistent and determined
Influencers	Story tellers, influencers
Self-confident	Self-confident
Knowledgeable about their product	Passionate and knowledgeable
Good networkers	Sociable with good verbal skills
Systematic about monitoring and review	(Can be learned)
Problem solvers	Atypical problem solvers
High standard setters	(Can be learned)

This is a very high level of convergence between these attributes. When you add to this what dyslexic adults need, then it may come as no surprise that so many of them choose self-employment.

Entrepreneurs need...	Successful dyslexic adults need...
High achievement	Achievement driven by passion
Autonomy	Choices and flexibility to deploy coping strategies
Space to pursue own views	Space for strengths to emerge
Power	

As can be seen, the needs of both groups overlap but there are also some differences in their drives.

Dyslexics may not have managerial competencies but can learn those

The really interesting aspect of comparing these lists is that the successful dyslexic adults have the innate characteristics required for entrepreneurial activity. The ones they may be missing – high standard setting and monitoring and review – are really managerial competencies which can easily be acquired.

Power can be destructive, and dyslexics may not crave it

On the input list, it is also of note that the dyslexic adults may come at this without the need for power. As power can be quite a destructive driver, it is possible that the dyslexic entrepreneur will find the ability to work in a team and to be empathetic to others. This will actually be a real strength when their business grows and matures.

Case study: Anna Devin

Irish soprano Anna Devin is widely admired for her 'vivid sense of bel canto style' (**The Arts Desk**), 'vocal control… artistry and musico-dramatic intelligence' (**Opera News**). Over the last few years she has established an international career, with appearances at Covent Garden, Carnegie Hall, Salzburg Festival and La Scala, to name a few.

Anna was diagnosed with dyslexia by 6 years of age, as her mother realised she was not reading as well as her older sister but was bright. She moved to

Alexandra College where the principal teacher was initially convinced that it was just that she wasn't trying hard enough in English lessons. She was kept back a year, during which she received good remedial lessons in literacy and proudly learned to spell Czechoslovakia, about which she now says, 'Typical, it doesn't exist now!'

Music always made sense, though, and she started learning to play the piano at 6, had recorder classes at 9, clarinet at 13 and singing throughout. Anna is still in touch with her first singing teacher, who led the school choir every week and suggested that Anna go in for competitions in her native Ireland. She always won a place in these competitions. Listening to her mother's Mozart C.D.s and then attending **The Marriage of Figaro** gave her a real affinity with opera. At age 13 and then again at 18, when she sang a solo from **The Messiah**, she represented her school in the National Concert Hall in Dublin. She maintained her singing lessons throughout, but at 18 decided that she ought to pursue a less risky and more lucrative career and went to university to study for a degree in the Science of Multi-Media. Sitting in the university library, attempting to re-read a particular book for the umpteenth time, Anna wondered why she had come to try to do something that made her feel ill. So, she went to see her singing teacher and asked her if she was good enough to pursue singing as a career. She postponed her degree course, and attended sessions at the Royal Academy of Music in Dublin. Shortly afterwards, she embarked on a 4-year music degree there, followed by 2 years on the opera course at the Guildhall

School of Music and Drama, then study at the National Opera Studio. After her study she was accepted onto the prestigious Jette Parker Young Artists Programme at the Royal Opera House, Covent Garden, which launched her career.

Anna has an exceptional ear for music, but it has not all been plain sailing. Opera is harder than instrumental music because of the languages. You need not only to learn the words in Italian, German or French but also you must understand the text so well that you can communicate the connection with the story and its emotions to the audience. She is a hard worker and the study at the Opera Studio was intense with 1-to-1 coaching in singing for 4 hours every day. At Covent Garden she received 1-to-1 German and Italian lessons and was surprised when her teachers told her she was very good at languages. This new knowledge helped her become aware of how important it was to know 'how you learn' and taught her to look for the best methods that suited her brain. To this day, she reads the text out loud and then writes it down and practises on the way to work. Movement is important to her too and she relies in part on where she is standing on the stage to assist her memory. 'I have a gift but I have worked very hard to hone it. I must share it. I love singing and it is completely liberating, it takes away the dyslexic self-critic inside me and allows language to be my friend rather than my enemy.'

Singing is a great joy to Anna but also brings joy to others. One man on hearing her sing one night said,

'I've had the worst week of my life but hearing you sing puts it all in perspective.' Her passion is to connect with others and get them to connect with themselves at this very deep emotional level. 'There is a moment between the audience and the performer that's amazing and you can't re-create it any other way.' It's an art form that encompasses the visual, auditory, kinaesthetic and affective elements in us which is the most powerful form of communication there is. 'Dyslexia is not a disability for me; it has taught me how to cope with things and more about myself.'

Key points from this chapter

★ Passion is about having joy in your life.

★ You must have a passionate interest to maintain motivation.

★ Passion for a topic is often what has led dyslexic individuals to learn to read.

★ You can refresh your passions in life.

★ Entrepreneurs are passionate about their undertakings.

★ There are significant overlaps between the competencies for an entrepreneur and a successful dyslexic person.

Chapter 4

You Need to Find Your Niche

'To each there comes in their lifetime a special moment when they are figuratively tapped on the shoulder and offered the chance to do a very special thing, unique to them and fitted to their talents. What a tragedy if that moment finds them unprepared or unqualified for that which could have been their finest hour.'

Winston S. Churchill

Definition of niche

If you look for a definition of 'niche' you may find something like: 'A shallow recess, especially in a wall to display a statue or other ornament' or 'A comfortable or suitable position in life or employment, a calling or vocation'. I particularly like the concept of the niche being something in a wall to display something beautiful or valuable. It paints a wonderful picture for me of a dyslexic person who is taking a central position in their environment and is highly valued for some particular ability.

Finding your niche is important

There is no doubt that the successful dyslexic adults in research studies had found a niche for themselves. McNully in 2003 identified in 'Dyslexia and the life course' that finding your niche in early adulthood can be transformational for those with dyslexia. If we think of any of the really famous dyslexic people we will see immediately that they also tended to operate in occupational niches that particularly suited them.

Matching you to the job

There is a theory called 'optimum match for jobs'. This occurs where the job requirements so closely match the individual's strengths that it's a marriage made in heaven!

Increases performance and self-esteem

Finding your own particular niche will increase your self-esteem, bringing you joy and satisfaction. If it's in the work environment, because you will perform well within it, bosses and colleagues will be forced to overlook your challenges because you will simply be so valuable to them for your strengths. What a result!

Finding your niche job or hobby

We are going to focus in this chapter largely on finding your niche job, but the techniques also apply to finding your niche hobby or community engagement.

Career planning

Despite the fact that our jobs and careers are extremely important to us in life, very few people receive career planning advice. Research by the Chartered Institute of Personnel and Development some years ago established that individuals arrive in their first job usually as a result of the outcomes of their school education, geographical location and family influence. In other words, the individual hasn't generally engaged very actively in working out what they might actually want to do and be best suited for.

What are you looking for?

You are likely to have started work on this process already, as the first question to ask yourself is 'What is your purpose in life? What are your values and passions?' There's that word again, passion – it keeps cropping up doesn't it? It's crucial that you find a niche that you can connect to emotionally in a good way as that will keep you determined and motivated and bring you joy.

Learn more about yourself

It's difficult to be completely objective about ourselves, our talents or how other people see us. The first stage in looking for a job or career that will suit you is to learn more about yourself. There are lots of free online tests that will tell you more about your personality, motivation and behaviour. These include the R.I.A.S.E.C. and Myers–Briggs tests, which are used extensively by career planners and recruiters, for example:

www.whatcareerisrightforme.com

http://personality-testing.info/tests/RIASEC

www.truity.com/test/type-finder-research-edition

www.careerfaqs.com.au/careers/career-personality-test

Job choices

Work changes all the time and jobs develop. Who would have thought even 10 years ago that our pattern of shopping would change so much that it is estimated that over the next decade the number of jobs for sales assistants will halve? On the plus side, though, the number of jobs that will maintain websites and electronic installations will increase significantly.

So the next stage is to research what jobs exist now and are likely to be around for some time to come. There is a huge amount of information online about types of jobs, average salaries and estimated growth in those industries. Here are some links, which list occupations in the U.K., U.S.A. and Australia, to get you started:

www.careerprofiles.info/careers.html

www.careerfaqs.com.au/careers/find-a-career

www.onetonline.org/find

Picking the right job for you

Once you have matched your talents and preferences to the available job choices, there are some practical questions which will help you to prioritise your choice:

- Have you got transferable skills for your job choice?

- If you need to do some additional training, is this an option for you?

- Will you earn enough to cover your bills?

- Are these jobs within your commuting distance?

- Will you have to relocate, and is this possible?

- Will the new job affect your family or their choices?

- Is this job going to be stable or risky, and are you comfortable with that?

Choosing to work in the right environment

Adults with dyslexia are happier in employment where there is general awareness of these conditions and some flexibility to deploy coping strategies. It has been shown that smaller employers generally are able to be more flexible around implementing reasonable adjustments and tend to appreciate the person for their individual strengths. So, not only is the choice of job important, but so is the environment in which you will work. The problem is finding out in advance whether this will be a good place to work in or not.

Dyslexia-friendly workplaces

There are not very many employers who advertise their workplace as dyslexia-friendly. In the U.K., there are quite a lot of firms with dyslexia networks internally but these are usually run by staff on a voluntary basis. You can read about one of these in the case study in Chapter 7 by John Levell.

The B.D.A. does have a kite mark, which is given to those organisations which pass the standards for a dyslexia-friendly workplace, and it is possible to ask for details on these by contacting the Charity at: Qualitymark@bdadyslexia.org.uk.

One of the best ways to find out how likely an organisation is to be supportive is to ask around, particularly of people who work there already. You may be able to find these people by following others on Twitter or looking people up on LinkedIn.

Government interventions for disability-friendly employment

There are initiatives by governments to extend and improve the experience of individuals with disabilities in employment. This is in their interests as it helps the economy if more people are in work.

In the U.K., the 'two ticks' scheme is currently in operation. Organisations registered under this scheme have committed to interview anyone applying for a vacancy who indicates they have a disability (and dyslexia is recognised as a disability in law for this purpose). The U.K. government has now launched the 'Disability

Confident' scheme which will replace the two ticks version. The government's aim is to get 50 per cent of disabled people into work.

In the U.S.A., in March 2014, there was an addition made to the law to encourage companies to be more proactive about hiring people with disabilities. The 'Final Rule' of Section 503 of the Rehabilitation Act of 1973 requires all government agencies, all companies with federal contracts, and any company that has a business relationship with a company that gets money from the federal government, to strive for a workforce which is at least 7 per cent made up of people with disabilities.

How to get your dream job

When you have decided what you'd really like to do as a job, then there may be a time-consuming period before getting it. Here are some ideas on how to go about it:

- Do some training to fill any gaps in your knowledge. You could look at M.O.O.C.s (massive open online courses). These are free, online and cover an astonishing range of topics.

- Get help to improve your C.V. It will appear to someone else as it will to a recruiter, so take note of any comments.

- Change your cover letter for every job you apply for, so that you can emphasise the points that they are looking for. You will find these in the 'the successful applicant will…' part of the advert or the person specification, if it is published.

- Apply for lots of jobs. This could be in the hundreds at least, before you find the one that happens to be an exact match for what you require and your skills set.

- Use all available networks to find out about potential and actual vacancies. These networks include your family and friends, any contacts on social media, recruitment companies and online job boards, and professional networks.

- You could also apply to do some volunteering in organisations that interest you.

Procrastinating – barriers to getting on with job hunting

We've all been there: it makes absolute sense to follow a course of action, but we don't. This is particularly true of trying to find your special niche. You know it would be good for you but there are lots of reasons why you don't get started or you flag part-way through. Here are some of the reasons why that happens:

- Fear of the unknown.

- It's too much work.

- I don't even know where to start.

- I have so much on already, I haven't got time to do another thing.

- I'm too old to change jobs now.

- There are very few jobs out there, I'm safe where I am.

- I don't have the necessary qualifications to do what I'd really like to do.

These are all perfectly reasonable and understandable barriers to change. You can decide to tackle them, though, if you value the prize of the niche that you would thrive in:

- Make one small change – it might help you where you are now. Remember, all journeys begin with a single step.

- Enlist the help of a friend or, even better, get a mentor to keep you motivated and reminded of the ultimate prize.

- Recognise that everyone is afraid of some changes, so this fear is normal but doesn't have to be paralysing.

- It's never too late to make positive changes in your life. If you are older, then start planning for the niche you might want to create for yourself in retirement. Healthy retirement is about doing something different, not retiring from life altogether.

- Review Chapter 1 on determination and motivation to see what else might work to get you started and keep you going.

Self-employment: examples of niche businesses

Your niche is likely to be a bit unusual because most of the obvious market opportunities tend to be taken by existing organisations looking to expand or change their product direction. So let's have a look at a few niche businesses that have been successful, to see the pointers we can learn from them.

Zumiez

Zumiez in the U.S.A. produce products relating to surfing, skate-boarding and snow-boarding. Here is what they say in 'About Zumiez':

> We made our debut in the Seattle area in 1978, with a single store location in Northgate Mall. Now we have grown, and currently have hundreds of stores across the United States and Canada. We do what others have only dreamed of! We provide you with cutting edge clothing, footwear, accessories, D.V.D.s, hard goods for skate and snow for active lifestyles. Everything we do revolves around the customer – you are the heart of our company. We love and support the skate and snow industries that our customers live and ride for.

Zumiez was started by Tom Campion, who knew of people in need in his neighbourhood. He wanted to help them out and started informally giving them food and clothes. As the company grew, they were able to set up a Foundation which is still giving out to people in hot and cold weather areas.

This is a story based heavily on the values and philosophy of the founder. Tom says, 'It's about the leverage, creating it and using it for the benefit of others and, in the process, of ourselves.' So we can learn from this that our niche should, perhaps, reflect our values and our philosophy on how the world works.

Gumbusters

Gumbusters operate out of New York and New Jersey in the U.S.A. They value eco-friendliness and also recognised that people didn't like chewing gum stuck to their carpets or the pavements. So they researched and patented their Gumcart, which only uses 4–8 gallons of water (far less than previous competitors) and no harsh chemicals.

These entrepreneurs worked on what was important, not just to them but also to their potential customers. They are using their view that eco-friendliness is an important factor in life and have built their business to incorporate this value. However, they had also spotted that no one wants gum on their shoes!

Guzman y Gomez and Mad Max

In Australia, some entrepreneurs identified a gap in the market for fresh, authentic Mexican food and now there are Guzman y Gomez and Mad Max, with both franchises spreading rapidly across the continent. Again, this was about a product that the entrepreneurs enjoyed and had identified a market gap which people would be willing to pay for.

SEEK

Finally, demonstrating the same points and also in Australia but operating across most of Asia now too, we have SEEK, whose 'About us' says:

> This is a diverse group of companies that have a unified purpose to help people live more fulfilling and productive working lives and help organisations succeed.

They operate in the traditional field of recruitment but they have also developed SEEK Learning, which has helped over 600,000 students find career-related education, and SEEK Volunteer which is a free service to not-for-profit organisations and in Australia the largest single source of volunteer opportunities.

We can see clearly from these examples that the values of the entrepreneurs have been built into the bedrock of their organisations.

Your talents and skills

So beyond what your values are, we next need to look at your talents and skills. What talents and skills do you have and which of these do you most enjoy using? From the ones that you enjoy, are there any that people would be willing to pay enough for? Remember, we don't want to fall into the trap of doing something we're passionate about but no one else wants.

Spotting gaps in the market

In thinking about possible products or niches, is there a real problem out there that isn't being solved? Is there something out there that isn't being done well enough? The answers to these two questions may give you a niche to pursue.

Entrepreneurialism is a state of mind. Once you get into the way of thinking that you can spot gaps, or 'me-too' products or services that you could improve, you will start to see business opportunities all over the place. So now we need a way of cutting these ideas down to something workable. Here are some things to ponder.

Gated markets

If your talents allow you to, choose something that is not easy for everyone to do. It might be that you need a qualification to offer a particular service, such as food hygiene if you want to offer a food service. These are opportunities with barriers to entry into the market. The higher the barrier to entry the less risk you have of being overcome by competitors. Here's a quick idea to test the competition: do an internet search on your product or service; if you get few hits, you know there are not that many people out there offering it. This is good for low competition, but think further about why there are few people offering it – is this something hard to do?

Choosing the best idea

Of your ideas, which one is the killer one that the most people are going to be willing to pay for? You will need to charge enough for all the activities your product or service will cost to bring to market, not just the gross amount you can earn.

What are the risks?

What risks are you facing? You will have to leave your comfort zone to do this but it's better to learn as you go along, so what you really want is something just outside your comfort zone.

Common traps to avoid

It is a real challenge to go into a self-employed venture. Often people do it because they have been made redundant and so they might as well try, and sometimes that brings them a richness they never expected. Here are some ideas about avoiding common traps that mean you never get off the couch with your idea!

- **Don't wait for the most auspicious moment.**
  There is no such thing as the perfect moment.
  When you are as sure as you can be that this is the right thing to do, then go for it. The danger here is that you will lose pace and the opportunity will be lost or taken up by somebody else.

- **Avoid the paralysis of over-analysis!** It's really important to do the research on the market, on the viability of your ideas. However, when we feel we are potentially engaging in something that makes us uncomfortable, because of the risks involved, we may engage in distracting behaviour, such as over-analysing all the figures.

Case study: Jonty Hearnden

Jonty Hearnden is one of the most recognisable faces on British T.V. when it comes to antiques and collectables. His T.V. career began in 1997 when he became one of the experts on the **Antiques Roadshow**. The programme is very popular in the U.K. and is now on its 38th series. Shows in the U..SA. and Canada have been developed from its successful formula. Jonty is also well-known for his many appearances on B.B.C.1's **Cash in the Attic**, **Celebrity Cash in the Attic** and **Put Your Money Where Your Mouth Is**, thus appearing almost daily on British television. He is one of our best examples of a dyslexic adult who has found a niche, several times over, and created a highly successful career.

He was born just outside London, in Brentwood. The family moved shortly after Jonty was born and he was brought up in the more rural and smarter area of a market town in Oxfordshire. He was identified as being dyslexic as a child and learned to deal as best as he could with his dyslexia while at school at Shiplake College. He says,

'I overcompensated for things I wasn't good at, like reading, by applying myself to the things I was good at, believing that I would succeed. I was good at sport, so played rugby and rowed at a competitive level.' He left school at 18 with A levels but thought tertiary education wasn't something he was good enough for.

Jonty's career started when he got a job at Bonhams Auctioneers, London. He applied himself to learning all he could about the antiques he was moving and cataloguing. He really liked it at Bonhams but after 10 months the auction house faced financial difficulties and he was made redundant. He then travelled the world for 10 months, very much enjoying visiting so many countries and diverse landscapes. Back home again, he phoned Bonhams and they gave him a job immediately. However, the pay was bad and Jonty realised that he didn't want to be on a very low income for ever. So he started thinking about what he could do to ensure that he earned more in future. This was the first example of Jonty using his diverse thinking skills and entrepreneurialism to achieve what he wanted in a slightly unusual way.

He realised that there were issues about the transportation of antique furniture and paintings. Mobile phones had just been developed and so he set up a transport business where he could be in touch with customers, buyers and the auction houses by mobile phone from his van. He ran the transport business for 6 years, employing up to 8 people. He was then approached by the owner of the Lots Road Gallery who wanted to take a sabbatical. Jonty sold his transport business and went to manage the Lots Road auction room. Then the owner returned from sabbatical so Jonty was forced by circumstance to reinvent his working life again and he set up and ran a successful antiques business, Dorchester Antiques, specialising in 18th and 19th century furniture and decorative objects. After 15 years of running Dorchester Antiques, recession hit the U.K. markets, people were buying far fewer antiques and Jonty was spending more and more of his time filming. So he sold the business.

He got into filming through a friend who approached him to go on the **Antiques Roadshow**. This led to him becoming a presenter on **Cash in the Attic**. This popular show ran for 26 series and the brand was sold to 145 countries. Filming wasn't always straightforward, though. The format of **Cash in the Attic** saw Jonty rummaging around the house of a contestant looking for hidden antiques which were then sold at auction with the proceeds going to the homeowner. During one episode, Jonty spotted a nice tea set but also noticed a musty smell coming from a fake Persian rug. Unfortunately, the rug was found to contain a decomposed body!

As the market changed again, Jonty and the show launched a website that provided expert valuations for a small fee. This way, if people were unsure of the current value of art work they own, they could upload a photograph of the item with a description and gain an expert evaluation. One art-lover discovered that his painting by urban artist Banksy, which he had bought a decade before for £5000, was now estimated to be worth up to £150,000.

However, throughout his career, dyslexia was always an issue and he tried his best to hide it. At an event at the Unicorn School, Jonty heard Sir Jackie Stewart speak. He found his talk inspirational and thought to himself that if Sir Jackie was dyslexic but had achieved so much, then it was O.K. to be dyslexic. Jonty shared his dyslexia with Angela Rippon (a journalist and newsreader). She knew his work and encouraged him to be more confident and be open about his dyslexia.

Ten years ago, Jonty trained as a business coach with the Henley Business School, but he also started a new enterprise. He has become a well-known charity auctioneer and M.C. working with many of the U.K.'s leading charities. He compiled a collection of signed modern and contemporary art and lithographs. These include signed pieces by names such as Picasso, Chagall, Miro, Emin, Banksy, Matisse, L.S. Lowry and Dali. These are sold at charity fundraising events. 'You did such a wonderful performance last night at our Williams F1 event, we have raised lots of money for our vital work with the most needy and vulnerable children' (Save the Children).

Jonty says, 'The best thing I did was to come to terms with my dyslexia and disability. In doing so I saw an opening and took a chance. I think sideways. I think about where I want to go and if I can't do it directly, I find other ways to get there. This different dyslexia thinking style, seeing the big picture, may not be exclusive to dyslexic people, but it is a trait many of them have. I think that it would be good to have 2 or 3 people with this thinking style on the Boards of companies. They would have a different way of thinking that is innovative and refreshing. Those individuals are often dyslexic and this would create an opportunity for using dyslexic people in a different and productive way.'

Key points from this chapter

★ All successful dyslexics have found their niche.

★ Your niche should be grounded in your values, passion and philosophy for life.

★ You need to analyse your talents and skills, and where you may need to upskill for a future venture.

★ Choose from the talents you most enjoy.

★ Look for either a gap in the market or an opportunity to do something that is being done, but much better.

★ Make sure the thing you choose is something others would and can choose to pay for.

★ Avoid activities where there are lots of existing competitors and no barriers to entry into the market.

★ Avoid the traps that stop you reaching for the skies.

Chapter 5

You Need to Use Your Atypical Problem-Solving Skills

'Dyslexics often have a different way of looking at things, and that difference can sometimes lead to interesting results.'

Geoff Blackwell

Research about atypical problem solving in dyslexics

In my research, the majority of participants were quite clear that they believed their dyslexia had endowed them with some special abilities. Top amongst these were atypical problem solving and several provided examples of this. Interestingly, this is not discussed or examined in much of the research on adults. However, if you are in a room with lots of dyslexic people, you will definitely find that the quality of solutions to problems is considerable and that the only impediment to solving the problem may be that all the energy is going into generating the solutions and not so much into moving on and choosing the right one!

It seems that dyslexic individuals are often really good at generating lots of solutions. In lay terms, the signals in a dyslexic person's brain may go around a wider and more complex circuit than in a non-dyslexic person. It is thought that this enables the opportunity for unusual connections to be made within the brain.

Techniques for problem solving

There are many techniques that have been developed for effective problem solving. Each different discipline, from medicine to engineering, has industry-based methodology that fine-tunes the way to approach and solve problems. However, most of these methods share the same basic approach:

- Identify and clearly describe the problem to be solved.

- Gather as much information as possible.

- Generate solutions.

- Select the best solution.

- Implement the solution.

- Monitor what happens, review and evaluate what worked.

Concept mapping to increase solutions

If you feel you need to develop the range of your generation of solutions, then engage in some concept mapping. There are a number of really good software programs and apps for concept mapping, so if this is your preferred way of working then there will be more information on these in the section on assistive technology in Chapter 9. However, many dyslexic individuals are quite happy to do this manually as you can adapt your map to contain visual clues or pictures or just use short words or abbreviations. It really doesn't matter what the spelling is like either!

To create a concept map, you need a large sheet of paper and some coloured pens or crayons. In the middle of the paper, write or draw the problem. As you start to come up with ideas, draw a line from the problem outwards and add your idea to the end of it. Our minds often work by association of ideas and so one thought you have may well lead to another, and before you know it your paper is covered in related ideas and connections.

Indicating connections on the map

There are some sophistications you can add to your concept map. If you feel the connection between one idea and another is strong, you can draw a broad line between them. Conversely, if you feel it's a weak connection, then you can draw a narrow line.

Numbering themes on the map

Subsequently, you can use a numbering method to work out how many themes you have on your map. So everything under one topic carries a 1, and then a 2 for the next topic. This is a really good way of ordering your ideas and your mind, which can be a critical skill for many on the dyslexia spectrum. Once the topics are grouped you can then decide on the priority of them and use an alphabetical code to denote priority. So the most important might be A and then B and so on down the priority order. As you may appreciate, concept mapping is a really useful tool for this and, indeed, in other circumstances too.

Settling on the best solution

However, allied to this very creative, divergent thinking is the need to settle on what the best solution is. This requires a different style of thinking and may be an area in which some adults need to develop more skill. This is about effective decision making, which we will now explore.

No absolute best

The first important point to stress is that it is fruitless to look for the absolute best solution as the chances are you will never identify it at the time. When we make decisions we are operating with the best information to hand, but it's not necessarily all the information about this topic. We've all experienced the feeling that 'if only I had known that at the time, I would have…' or 'with the benefit of hindsight…' So, our objective is to make the best decision we can at the time.

Evaluating solutions

The way we go about making a choice is to use some method to evaluate the options. This can be as simple as weighing up the pros and cons. For choices with potentially serious outcomes we develop the pros and cons model into an evaluation model with more criteria. To explore this let's take the example of making a decision to buy a new car. There are lots to choose from so we are quite used to coming up with several criteria to cut down the choice, as follows:

My new car must have:

- room for 4 people

- good visibility through the back window for reversing

- an engine powered by petrol

- 4-wheel drive

- an appropriate price.

You would probably add several more criteria to the list if you were really considering buying a new car.

Weighting criteria

We can extend this model further by weighting the criteria. Some of these things will be more important to us than others. So we might, for example, say if I can get all these features in more than one car, then the price might be more important to me than other things, in which case I will give that a weighting of double the other criteria. This concept of weighted evaluation is used a lot in work situations. Sometimes we construct a decision matrix so that we can see all the key issues and calculate their weighting, at a glance. Here is an example of that, based on recruiting a new member of staff.

Candidates	Proficiency in using office software	Weighting 4	Experience of managing staff	Weighting 2
J. Banks	Novice	4	Strong	2
B. Field	Expert	4	None	2
W. Meadow	Expert	4	Good	2

We can see from this evaluation that W. Meadow is probably the best person for the job, as whilst J. Banks has stronger management experience, their proficiency in IT is weaker and the weighting indicates the importance placed on IT compared with management experience.

Costs and benefits

Quite often our evaluation includes financial information and we frequently talk about 'cost–benefit analysis' in organisations. This is just another example of a criteria-based decision method. We look at all the costs and list all the benefits so we can decide whether the benefits are worthwhile for the financial investment.

Hard and soft data

This raises an interesting perspective on decision making. Some background information is hard data, whilst other information is about things that are either qualitative or hard to quantify (soft data). To illustrate, if we take the example above of recruiting a new person, it is relatively easy to assess an individual's skill in using some software as you can construct a test and observe how they perform. It is much more difficult to get accurate and sound information on how good they are as a manager. Decisions based on hard data, or a mix of hard data and soft data, can be felt to be more trustworthy than those only based on soft data or intuition.

Ethical decision making

Recently, in the wake of concerns about financial institutions and how they have made decisions, there has been a rise in interest about ethical decision making. I include this for our consideration because a lot of this rests on values, and this has been a key theme throughout this book. In the ethical decision-making model, filters are implemented at the stage of considering the solutions. So we can ask several questions of these potential solutions:

- Is the solution consistent with my values or, if within an organisation, its stated ethics and policies?

- Is the solution legal and does it meet industry regulatory standards?

- If we asked 95 per cent of the population whether this is a morally acceptable solution, what would they say?

- Do I feel that I can live with the consequences of this solution?

Ineffective decision making

There are some particular ways in which it is known that people do not make good decisions. These are:

- working with insufficient information about the problem

- paralysis caused by constantly looking for the 'right' solution rather than the best one with the available data

- not getting to the 'do it' stage but over-analysing everything.

Procrastination can be good

We can interpret paralysis, rather than getting on and implementing the best solution, as procrastination. There was also a study by Ferrari and Sanders (2006) where adults with A.D.H.D. (Attention Deficit Hyperactivity Disorder, which is genetically related to dyslexia) reported significantly higher levels of procrastination than other subjects who did not have A.D.H.D.

However, interestingly, there has been research recently that suggests that there is 'good' and 'bad' procrastination. Good procrastination is interpreted as being where although it may look like the individual is just not getting on with it (whatever 'it' is), they will suddenly come up with a fully formed and sophisticated solution. What they have been doing, in fact, is quietly brewing the result. Allowing time and the brain to work in a relaxed or sleep state on problems has been known for a long time to produce optimum conditions for decision making. This is what the good procrastinators are doing.

By contrast, of course, some individuals do procrastinate and they don't suddenly have solutions emerging like a butterfly from the chrysalis. If you are a procrastinator, you can still develop ways of working that will assist you. Here are a few key ones.

Prompts to avoid 'bad' procrastination

At the end of each working day, spend 5 minutes to construct your to-do list for the next day. Colour-code the list so that things that are important and urgent are identified in red, things that are important but not due yet are coloured orange, and those that are neither urgent nor important can be coloured blue (you may not get around to doing these but the penalty for not doing so is not very high).

The late afternoon is the very best time to do this list because you are in the moment – in the morning you will need to refocus yourself and remember all the details of things you have been working on that impact on your prioritising the list.

Set alarms on your mobile phone as a means of prompting you to get on with items. If this doesn't work for you, then ask a trusted colleague to remind or prompt you.

Think about when you work best and are likely to suffer the least amount of interruptions during the day. This is the time to allocate for your priority work if you can.

Emotional side of decision making

So, we now feel that we have a number of tools to enhance our decision making. Unfortunately, there is one more thing to learn and we definitely need to take account of it. Very recently, psychologists have been studying the emotional side of decision making. What they have found is that humans are not actually all that good at making rational decisions. Our decision-making activity is both a rational and an emotional activity. In many instances, the engagement of our emotions in our decision making is a good thing.

However, we have lots of biases that affect us and we are well advised to be aware of them. Many of these biases come about because our world is very complex and so we develop 'rules of thumb' that enable us to short-circuit the system and use our intuition.

Our bias

First there is our bias towards building all our views on the behaviours of very successful people and events. We study a very successful person and try to emulate them (don't worry – this book has been written from the perspective of people who are moderately successful as well as the very successful, otherwise we could be falling into this particular trap). Let's take the example of running a very successful event. Afterwards, we review all the things that worked and build that into a plan for running the next conference.

However, it only takes one thing to differ in the context of setting up the next conference for a chain reaction to build up which means our successful planning criteria turn the event from a success to a crisis. In a similar vein, there are lots of books written about 'How to make your first million' and 'How x built a conglomerate'. These are written on the basis that if we emulate these individuals' behaviours we will also make a million. However, we usually can't replicate the circumstances they were in exactly, and so we may not achieve the goal.

Loss aversion

We value the things we have now, and whilst we may want a slight improvement in our situation, we are more focused on avoiding losses. This loss aversion makes us risk-averse and so we may consider decisions in the light of potential risk of loss. That makes us choose the less risky option rather than going with the best solution according to the available data. As an example of this, suppose your current job doesn't offer you any development or excitement but it's enough to pay your mortgage. You are offered a more senior job, with more money, but you fear that you may lose the companionship of your colleagues and you may at a later date have to travel more. So you make your 'rational' decision that you are better off staying in your current and safe job.

We tend to overvalue the things we know about and underestimate the effects of things we don't know about.

Valuing ranges rather than absolute numbers

We are affected by ranges of numbers rather than the absolute. Recently I was at the airport and realised I had left my sunglasses at home. In the duty-free shop, I was looking for a cheap pair of sunglasses to last me the week while I was away from home. Most of the sunglasses were for very well known brands and had, to my mind, high price tags. I then found some unbranded sunglasses which were still actually pretty expensive in absolute terms. However, because my brain had been influenced first by the much higher price, I considered the non-brand sunglasses to be good value. I had been influenced by the range of numbers rather than an absolute test of value.

Confirmation of our existing beliefs

We look for confirmation of our existing beliefs – this is called 'confirmation bias'. For example, you believe you are a particular type of person and you read a magazine article which discusses personality types. You will be inclined to ignore anything that does not match your view of yourself. We do this all the time, and it considerably affects our decisions.

Brexit as example

All of these biases could be seen in the discussions by ordinary U.K. citizens in the lead-up to the vote on whether the U.K. should leave or remain in the E.U. Many individuals, in describing how they had made their decision about how to vote, discussed what they might stand to lose if the U.K. remained or left the E.U.; however, individuals were taking more notice of those whose views generally accorded with them than of those who held contrasting views. The arguments put forward by both sides were widely criticised for inaccurate factual content. The whole campaign could be said to have been waged on the basis of affecting individuals' emotional states prior to them making their decision.

Be alert to bias

So, what can we do about this? Not an awful lot, as our brains are built with a decision-making process which

uses the emotional centre of the brain as well as
the rational area and all of it is heavily intertwined.
So the important thing may be to recognise and be
alert to biases in our judgement which will affect the
choices we make.

Case study: Geoff Blackwell

Geoff Blackwell is an acclaimed creator and publisher
of best-selling illustrated books. He publishes about
20 books per year in 30 countries. These are exquisite
photographic books. His authors have included icons
such as the late Nelson Mandela and Desmond Tutu,
along with some of the world's leading photographers –
a number of whom he has discovered are also dyslexic.

Geoff knew he was dyslexic from an early age and
had remedial lessons. However, he was 14 before a
long-distance trip and associated boredom and lack
of distractions led him to spend the necessary time to
learn to read fully. He dropped out of school in the sixth
form and went to work for his parents, who were also
publishers. Whilst he says he outgrew his dyslexia, anyone
who reads his story can see how his brain operates
differently. His solutions to problems are offbeat, creative.

How do you get over being dyslexic and going on
to publish books? He says, 'Easy: focus on photo books.'
His first big idea came from inspiration upon seeing
a reprint of a catalogue from the 1955 exhibition of
'The Family of Man', which was a compilation of over

500 pictures taken by 273 photographers worldwide. Geoff pitched his idea to modernise this concept to his then boss (his parents had sold the firm to Hodder). He proposed to launch one of the most ambitious international photography competitions ever staged, and to develop the project without being paid in return for the company financing the project and splitting the profits. The result, M.I.L.K. (Moments of Intimacy, Laughter and Kinship), was a huge international success drawing in 17,000 entries from 164 countries and becoming the basis for a touring exhibition and series of books that sold over 4 million copies.

More creative thinking resulted in a unique approach at the Frankfurt book fair. Geoff mocked up a film studio wrapped in reels with M.I.L.K. images and served publishers flat white coffees while they watched a slideshow. The success of M.I.L.K. enabled Geoff to set up his own publishing house, P.Q. Blackwell, in 2003. He now runs this with 20 staff in Auckland, New Zealand.

The M.I.L.K. exhibition toured to London and a representative of the Princess of Wales Memorial Fund saw it. Blackwell was approached to produce the first and only authorised portrait of Princess Diana's life. The foreword was written by Nelson Mandela, which gave Blackwell an introduction to him and he started a long and successful relationship with Mandela and a number of other South African authors including Desmond Tutu.

Inspired by the opportunity to work with humanitarian icons, Blackwell has continued to develop his publishing ideas, many of which have a philanthropic inspiration. His latest success has been founded on a bestselling series of cookbooks that raise money for food security organisations.

His advice to other dyslexics is to view it as a positive. 'Dyslexics often have a different way of looking at things, and that difference can sometimes lead to interesting results. Have confidence in your own ability and find out what it is you should be doing to make the most of your own unique talent.'

Key points from this chapter

★ Adults with dyslexia may be particularly good in generating atypical solutions to problems, though this is largely through anecdotal and observed behaviours rather than a wealth of research projects to support this view.

★ There are tools such as concept mapping that can help you develop a range of solutions.

★ Solutions can be weighted to help us make rational choices, and this can particularly help us with complex decision making.

★ Hard data is easier to evaluate than soft data.

★ Procrastination can be good if it enables the individual to develop the best solution in a relaxed way.

★ Decision making is not an entirely rational activity – emotions are always involved.

★ We have to be on the alert for biases whenever we make decisions.

Chapter 6

You Need to Make the Most of Your Creativity

'Everything you can imagine is real.'

Pablo Picasso

Creativity and dyslexia

Whilst it is a widely held view amongst the dyslexic community that dyslexia is associated sometimes with remarkable artistic creativity, this is very controversial. Why is this so? A study of creativity indicates some very interesting ideas.

In fact, very few academic studies confirm the link between creativity and dyslexia. It may be that this is due to an insufficiency of academic studies researching this area. It is also necessary in the research for the test of the hypothesis to be very carefully constructed in order to yield interesting and valid results. Whatever the reasons are, so far we do not have a conclusive, evidenced study confirming any link between the two areas.

However, one study has looked at the prevalence of art students with dyslexia difficulties compared with non-art students (Wolff and Lundberg 2002). This found that the incidence of dyslexia was higher amongst the art students. It may be, though, in this instance, that what we are seeing are individuals who have honed their skills in one particular area because they felt at a disadvantage in studies that required good literacy skills. However, personally, I do not feel this gives us the full picture so let's examine this from the beginning.

Creativity of preschool children

In studies done with preschool children, they are shown to be capable of great creativity. However, by the time they are 11, only 1.6 per cent of them score as highly on tests of creativity. So to be still capable of creative thought as an adult is a very much needed ability. Somewhere in early childhood a lot of us are losing our creativity. So where does it go?

Left-brained or right-brained – it's a myth

I have frequently heard dyslexic artists say they are right-brain dominated. This concept that those with right-brain dominance are creative and emotionally centred, whereas those with left-brain dominance are rational and analytical, is a myth. It came about from studies done in the 1960s. The research was done on patients with severe epilepsy who were operated on to sever the cross-hemisphere connection. Post-operatively these patients do not represent normal brain activity. We now know that both hemispheres in the brain are inextricably linked. Creativity involves many cognitive processes, neural pathways, our emotions and memory.

Do we know how the brain works for creativity?

The reality is that we know relatively little about the operation of the brain. Additionally, whenever we learn more, it also teaches us how complex it is and how much more we have to learn! Why is it so difficult to examine the brain? After all, we have some extremely sophisticated technology now such as Positron Emission Tomography (P.E.T.) scans and functional magnetic resonance imaging (f.M.R.I.). Designing neuro-imaging studies, however, is extremely tricky. The average human brain has about 100 billion neurons (or nerve cells). These are connected to each other by billions of spines which contain the synapses. The synapses allow chemical or electrical signals to pass between neurons. A typical neuron fires 5–50 times per second. Therefore, it is not surprising that capturing brain activity using even sophisticated technology inevitably leads to oversimplifications. We're also not really sure what we are looking for, or where we are looking, when trying to track creativity.

Therefore, what follows is really only everyone's best guess about how it seems to work.

The creative process

We know that cultivating ideas and being creative is a process. There seem to be 3 possible variants:

- Simply combining things we knew already.

- Bringing things we know together but seeing them in a new relationship to each other.

- Learning something completely new to us and connecting that with what we knew already.

How we do this appears to be a process consisting of:

- collecting information for the brain to work upon

- manipulating the information

- producing something new (the 'aha' moment)

- evaluating ideas.

Now if you look at Chapter 5 about atypical problem solving, you will see that this is our old friend 'divergent thinking'. We know that dyslexics are good at this because their brains direct signals around a roundabout route enabling unusual combinations to occur. So is this another link to why dyslexic people state they are good at creativity?

How the brain achieves the creative process

We have already determined that creativity does not involve a single brain region or single side of the brain.

It results from the dynamic interactions of lots of brain areas that are called into action according to the task and operate in large-scale networks. One network is responsible for us really focusing on a task, but it should be noted that this puts heavy demands on working memory, which is often more difficult for those with dyslexia. This may partially explain why dyslexic adults tend to find congruent thinking, that is, choosing the best solution, more difficult to do.

A second network is thought to be responsible for constructing thoughts on previous experiences, empathy and generating alternative scenarios. This is the area that we believe dyslexic adults are particularly good at.

Finally, a third network monitors things that are happening to us and our stream of consciousness; this controls which part of the brain is best for what task. When we allow the control area to relax, more ideas are allowed to flow. This may be why we come up with better ideas when we sleep on them!

The characteristics of creative individuals

There have been lots of studies on creative people, just not on dyslexic creative people. These studies have tended to point to individuals who are:

- curious, adventurous

- willing to take risks

- persistent and determined

- passionate and potentially compulsive over their particular interest

- resilient to criticism from others, so have sufficient self-esteem

- unconventional

- tolerant of disorder

- often self-taught and not successful in education systems.

Does this remind you of anyone or another list of characteristics? Interestingly, some of the case studies quoted in the research on creative individuals name people who are known to be dyslexic.

You don't have to be super-bright to be a creative genius

One of the questions examined has been how bright you have to be to be really creative. In fact, there are lots of problems with using I.Q. tests, particularly in the area of creativity. I.Q. does not map easily onto improvements in anticipated life outcomes. The tests often don't work fully with dyslexic people because many rely on literacy. Tests are also subject to cultural differences. Additionally, how can you compare one person's creativity with another? It is much more personal than that, it's much more ipsative (i.e. looks at a range of individual factors in a person rather than comparing their scores with another person's). In conclusion, the research has led to the 'threshold theory' which holds that, above a certain level, intelligence doesn't have much effect on creativity.

Is creativity hereditary?

We know that dyslexia is inherited, but we don't know about creativity. It is certainly true that you get siblings who are creative. As examples, we have a whole family of Strauss (composers), Ben and Casey Affleck (actors), Beyoncé and Solange Knowles, Miley and Trace Cyrus, William and Wellington Grisa (software developers), Christopher and Peter Hitchens (authors and journalists). This takes us to the nature versus nurture argument: were they born with talents or were the conditions right as they grew up to nurture those talents?

Is there a link between creativity and mental health?

There are a lot of studies that have been done to see whether creative people are more prone to bipolar disorder, depression and mood swings. Whilst there are lots of examples that can be quoted, the research just isn't strong enough yet to establish whether a link exists. One thing we do know about mental health, though, is that it's not that healthy to brood and have negative thought patterns. A lot of creative people do need to have space and time to think to be creative. You may remember that in my research, many of the respondents advocated that young dyslexic people need to develop positive mindsets. Many dyslexic adults suffer from stress and there is considerable interest in health and wellbeing currently. However, as Tom Insel, head of the U.S. National Institute, said, 'Psychiatric disorders are massively, intimidatingly complicated.'

Creative success doesn't just happen

Therefore, while we would all like to think that creativity just happens, the studies show that this is not the case. Where huge breakthroughs are made, generally the creative thinker has extreme interest in their topic, has spent many hours thinking about it and is an expert. You can see this with examples such as Bell on the invention of the telephone and Edison on the invention of the light bulb (they had 1000 failures en route). Incidentally, Edison was told by teachers that he was 'too stupid to learn anything'. Creative success takes hard work, revision, failure, extensive knowledge and persistence.

However, being able to take in all the specifics in a given situation and spot patterns in a dynamic changing situation (which is a particular strength that some dyslexic adults have) is definitely a help to this process.

Examples of creativity by dyslexic individuals

So whilst the research may not yet back up the idea that creativity is linked with dyslexia, it is really interesting to look at the things that dyslexic individuals have created. While we often tend to think of creative people as being artists or actors, we have seen already that there are lots of ways of being creative. Maybe this gives us a different kind of evidence base. Here are some examples of other types of creativity by dyslexic adults. Our lives have all been touched by these individuals' inventions:

- The Wright Brothers were two American brothers and aviation pioneers. They are credited with inventing, building and flying the world's first successful airplane from North Carolina, U.S.A., in 1903. Whilst they were not the first to build and fly novel aircraft, they invented the first workable fixed-wing aircraft. Their invention of the 3-axis control, enabling the pilot to steer and maintain the aircraft's equilibrium, was a breakthrough. Interestingly, their approach was significantly different to other research at the time.

- Baruj Benacerraf, a Venezuelan-born American immunologist, received the Nobel Prize in Physiology with 2 colleagues in 1980. He had discovered the major histocompatibility complex genes which encode cell surface protein molecules important for the immune system's distinction between self and non-self. This has been an incredibly important building block for many areas of medicine, including transplant surgery and the treatment of autoimmune illnesses. Benacerraf attributed much of his success to having good spatial awareness, but it is also obvious that he worked with determination on his research.

- Walt Disney was an American film producer and animator. He created Mickey Mouse, Fantasia and Dumbo. He was the first person to introduce live action with animation. However, Disney was also obsessed with innovation and founded the Imagineering department. This has since been granted over 115 patents in special effects, interactive technology and fibre optics.

Find out how creative you are

If you are ready for a bit of light-hearted fun, you may want to try out the following quiz to see how creative your brain is already: www.shelleycarson.com/creative-brain-test.

Conformity stifles creativity

Conformity is the enemy of creativity. The process of conforming starts in school but it continues into work. If there were no agreed ways of working together, there would be conflict all the time! This is why we have grievance and disciplinary policies at work – they codify the ways in which we handle conflict. Other policies such as Health and Safety spell out the rules that we need to conform to in order to keep everyone safe.

However, these do not leave room for anyone to be creative. While these policies are very necessary for harmony and productivity, which we all desire, the downside is that if you spend a lot of your time conforming and also working at a job with lots of procedures which leave little scope for creativity (which is common), then the creative side of your personality can get rusty. Your brain just doesn't have to think in creative styles, but needs to practise in order to be versatile with different thinking styles. Here is how we can re-energise our creative thinking abilities.

Re-energising our creativity

Can you think of areas in which you are creative? If you are struggling for inspiration on this, ask a friend or partner about where they see you being creative.

Sometimes we don't see our own strengths – we tend to take them for granted (though we are usually very aware of our weaknesses!). It's very important to give due weight to our abilities. Maybe you will find that you need to unlock your creativity.

So to unlock, or re-energise, your creativity, you need to be freed up and do creative things more often. You need to find ways to collect information for the brain to work upon. Here are some ways you can start to do this:

- **Create some space in your life** when it's O.K. to do nothing or be creative.

- **Get some resources that you can make things with.** This could be blank paper for drawing, painting, craft or writing on. It could be bits of wood for making things, or material for sewing or knitting. It doesn't matter what you do as long as you feel free to experiment and, once you do that, your imagination will take over.

- **Learn to meditate.** This is easy and there are lots of guided meditations on YouTube to get you started. When your mind is free-flowing and relaxed (which is what meditation is all about), then new ideas will start to evolve without you consciously having to do anything.

- **Learn or do something completely different.** This will stimulate you to think about new things and encourage your brain to make new connections.

- **Use a concept map to do some 'blue sky thinking'.** In this you think about something you might want to do, such as to have an adventure, visit Nepal or Machu Picchu or anything else that attracts you. Jot or draw all the ideas you have; do not evaluate them or cross anything out until afterwards. This ideas generation is very creative and it's the later activity of evaluation that is different; the appropriate style of thinking for that is rational thinking.

If you are looking for additional stimulus then go to
www.ted.com/talks/tim_brown_on_creativity_and_play
for further ideas and activities.

Allow time to process the information and wait for the 'aha' moment

Once the brain has enough stimulating material,
you need to be able to trust it to do its best. As we
learned earlier, the brain is most active at creating the
connections essential to creativity when we are relaxed.
It doesn't work well when we are concentrating heavily
on the task before us or when it's exerting control on
our behaviours. So, we need to give it space to think
unconsciously. You cannot force the 'aha' moment of
inspiration or insight. In fact, we all know from experience
that our best such moments occur at the oddest times.
We wake up with a complete solution to a problem that
we had been tussling with all the previous day. Or we are
doing a mindless task, such as mowing the lawn, when
suddenly the light-bulb moment arrives!

The more ideas the better, but you need to evaluate them

Our brains are working all the time with thoughts flitting
in and out. The more stimulus we give ourselves, the
more ideas we will come up with. This is good – it's good
to have lots of ideas as some of them will be bad. So the
final stage in the creative process is to evaluate our ideas
and only select the good ones. This is exactly the same
process as we use in problem solving.

People are more creative outside work

A long time ago, I was asked to run an event for G.E.C. Marconi as it was a major anniversary for the company. This event was for the women who worked at their assembly plant in Rochester, U.K., and the theme was 'celebration'. I arrived for the evening and there were approximately 200 women gathered in a very large room, sitting in rows facing me. As an icebreaker, I had decided to ask these women to share 3 things they were proud of with the neighbours either side of where they were sitting. After this I asked for volunteers to share some of the things they were proud of.

The answers were astonishing and everyone had something they were proud of achieving. There was one lady who handmade costumes for a very well known and dramatic T.V. personality. Another lady said she was most proud of the fact that both her children were qualifying as doctors, even though she had not had much of an education before coming to Britain 30 years previously. I don't remember all the examples, although there were very many and it was incredibly inspiring. However, all these women were giving examples of creativity and achievement outside of the workplace. At work they were assembling machinery, which required extreme conformity.

During the Roffey Park research project (Lammiman and Syrett 2000), the authors describe how observing something very similar led to their research project. All the people they studied, they said, were extremely creative outside work in their hobbies and activities. However, this did not extend to work and they decided this was such an oversight for businesses that they needed to research how organisations could build in the factors that would allow creativity to flourish.

Creative thinking

We have already said earlier that whilst we tend to think of creativity as being about art, in the widest sense, in fact there really is a need for creativity in work and general living. In the previous chapter we looked at creative problem solving, how we can be very good at generating lots of diverse solutions to problems. If we study the role of creativity in work, we can learn a lot about how we might use our strengths in this area. This also overlaps with entrepreneurialism, and many dyslexic adults are successful entrepreneurs and can be 'intrepreneurs' (those who act as entrepreneurs within an organisation).

Creativity and entrepreneurs

In the work context, we can describe creativity as the occasional moment when the elements collide together to produce something sparkling and new. Ackoff (1978) said, 'Creativity is the ability to look at things in a new way.' It has been estimated that less than 0.02 per cent of individuals have entrepreneurial capabilities (I don't think they can have included the dyslexics!).

How creative teams work

We can examine significant examples of creative teams to uncover some of the foundation of their success. Watson and Crick worked together with Rosalind Franklin to discover the structure of D.N.A. They worked in a laboratory (so not a hugely glamorous environment); they worked odd hours (again not a factor in personal comfort). There were only 3 of them and a relatively small network of external contacts. They were completely passionate and committed to what they wanted to achieve (sounds like our old friends 'determination' and 'passion' at work here); they were competitive, strove to achieve their goal before others did, and they were very knowledgeable in their subject.

Terence Conran example

Much the same pattern applies to Terence Conran who set up Habitat and created lifestyle shopping, which is still important in retail today. He couldn't get others to accept his ideas. He was very passionate about furnishing style so he set up his own shop. He had a small team, was committed to an idea, was knowledgeable about furniture and design, and was an achiever. We can see these features again and again if we study fashion houses, advertising agencies, research and development teams and others.

Innovation

Innovation, that blend of creativity and implementation, is seen as crucial to business sustainability and growth.

Admittedly, we don't need unfettered creativity – the business world is littered with examples of organisations that got it wrong. So it is important that creative, innovative initiatives take place within the context of the overall business plan. Therefore, what works is some separation of creative solution generation from the evaluation and implementation stages, but both creative thought and process skills are important and valuable.

Creative process at work

Within the work context, the creative process works a bit like this. Either through imagination or faced with a challenge or a problem to solve, the mind continuously and unconsciously processes information. Often resonance or association with earlier thinking produces a new idea, the 'aha' phenomenon.

Creative dyslexics

It's particularly interesting looking at this through the lens of dyslexic entrepreneurs. They are always passionate about their ideas. They become extremely knowledgeable about their area of interest and expertise. At least at the beginning, they tend to work alone or in small groups. Is there something in the spark that led to them working outside traditional organisations due to them not being able to be successful within an organisation? Probably so, and that means that we are missing out both at an individual level, as not all adults with dyslexia want to build their own businesses, and as a society. Which begs the question of how the creativity of adults with dyslexia can be harnessed to everyone's benefit.

Working in a creative team

It's rare to hear about one creative person working in a silo within a large organisation. What we see is people working in creative teams. We can learn a lot by observing common traits in these teams. In 2003, as part of the European Space Agency's Mars Mission, a consortium led by Professor Pillinger designed and built Beagle 2. The principal members of this team and their responsibilities were: Open University as the team lead and responsible for scientific experiments; University of Leicester for project management; Astrium as the main industry partner; Martin Baker for the entry and re-entry systems; Logica and SCISYS for specialist software; and University of Wales, Aberystwyth, for the robotic arm.

You only had to watch the team on television at the time describing what they were doing, to see their enthusiasm. They demonstrated the traits we expect in such teams. They were enthusiastic and had a shared vision to which they were all committed. None of them could achieve the project alone, they were dependent on each other as all teams have to be. They were all committed to delivery; they had support overall for the innovation. Finally, communications between partners and the outside world had been carefully planned. Sadly, the project was not an overall success as the lander failed to open as planned on Mars. Nonetheless, there was a lot of learning that took place and future exploration will be influenced by the project.

Pitfalls of diversity

As we work more globally now, there are some pitfalls for creative teams working across cultures and languages. Working in different time zones and in different mother languages certainly can affect the communications within the team. Diversity was seen as a potential pitfall in a study by Schwarz (2015). This study related to racial diversity, but the lessons apply equally well to dyslexia. The issue identified was that where the team is diverse, there can be language and cultural barriers which foster misunderstanding. One of the key barriers individuals with dyslexia face is a lack of awareness of dyslexia. This could be easily addressed with awareness training of the key aspects of the condition, its prevalence throughout society and the ways in which individuals, dyslexic or otherwise, can work together to support each other.

Roles in ideas development

In 1999, Roffey Park Management School undertook a very large survey of senior managers about where they got their inspiration from (Lammiman and Syrett 2000). These managers came from 4 very different organisations: British Airways, Save the Children (U.K.), IntegriSys and Permanent Headquarters (U.K.). One of the really interesting conclusions, which is still highly relevant today, was to define the roles in ideas development (i.e. creativity) in these teams. The table shows that model.

Role	Definition	Undertaken by
Spark	Spots or comes up with ideas	Any employee or associate, often from unexpected areas
Sponsor	Promotes idea, ensures it's not dismissed	Senior managers, directors
Shaper	Fleshes out idea or makes it practical	Project team, process consultant, research and development staff from suppliers
Sounding board	Someone objective with broader knowledge	Professional networks, trusted senior colleagues, mentors, academics, etc.
Specialist	Specialists with very specific knowledge	Project team members, consultants, academics

This suggests that anyone with the appropriate skills can take on roles in creative teams and that dyslexia should be an advantage in some of them.

Summary

So to sum up, what we have learned is that creativity and innovation is essential within organisations. Creative teams need to operate within the overall aims of the organisation, but to get the best out of them you need to relax some organisational rules to give more latitude to working arrangements. We need to separate the creative thinking part from the implementation as procedural thinking does not sit well with creative thinking. There are distinct roles within creative teams and much of the knowledge and skills can be acquired for these.

The debate about whether creativity is an innate ability conferred by dyslexia takes on another view when we look at the requirements for being creative. There is little doubt that there is considerable overlap between the criteria for the creative process and the way dyslexic adults think. When you are recruiting for a particular job, you list the skills needed for it. If we were to list the skills needed for the creative process, we would be looking to recruit dyslexic adults!

Case study: Aakash Odedra

Aakash is an outstanding choreographer. He trained in the classical Indian dance styles of Kathak and Bharat Natyam. He performed at the Queen's Diamond Jubilee celebrations and the closing of the London Cultural Olympiad. He has won numerous awards and bursaries, including a Danza & Danza award (Italy), a Dora performance award (Canada) and a Sky Academy Arts scholarship. His dancing is beautiful and mesmeric.

Kathak dance means to tell a story. It comes from northern India and was inspired by Islamic poetry and Hindu stories. It may be the only art form to infuse these roots. Aakash takes the essence of this classical training but translates it into a communication which is accessible to all.

Until he was 21, he didn't realise that his name began with 2 'a's because of his dyslexia. He designed a dance, Murmur, to show others what it's like for him to be dyslexic and because it is a tough subject for many to disclose or discuss. Aakash says that dyslexia exists within the mind but affects the physical and your outlook or perception. In order to share that perception with others, it is necessary to delve into the world of imagination. The piece is called Murmur because when you have starlings which fly, they make formations which warp and change; they baffle the mind. This is what it was like for Aakash at school where letters would change – they would make sense in his mind but be illogical to others when he wrote. He describes how when you look at something when you are dyslexic, it changes, it morphs. You can demonstrate that by using technology. So in the dance, the technology shifts from a simple paper thrower to complex technology which can sense his movements across the floor. Papers with letters on are flown by fans.

Aakash says, 'Dyslexia has a negative connotation but for me it is a blessing. It means that I look at the world in a different way, I interpret things differently. There is nothing wrong with being different, it's an advantage and that's what Murmur is about. It's a dance with a new freshness, a new dynamic to it to communicate what dyslexia can feel like.'

Key points from this chapter

★ Whilst anecdotally people believe that many dyslexic individuals have particular strengths in creativity, we do not have the academic research to prove this. However, there is some research which shows that more people studying art have dyslexia than those studying non-art courses.

★ The characteristics of creative people look very much like many of the characteristics shared by dyslexic individuals.

★ Creativity is present in many different arenas, it is not limited to the 'art world'.

★ Conformity and procedures can be an impediment to creativity.

★ Creativity is a process which requires practice.

★ There are activities you can do to increase your creative thinking powers.

★ Creativity links with entrepreneurialism.

★ Creative teams are essential to business and there are different roles within these teams, and it is possible to develop the attributes for many of these roles.

★ Dyslexia is one type of diversity, along with race and culture, in which team members may need sensitivity training, so they can operate best.

Chapter 7

You Need to Go with Your Empathy

'You never really understand a person until you consider things from his point of view, until you climb inside of his skin and walk around in it.'

Atticus Finch in To Kill a Mockingbird *by Harper Lee*

Grit or empathy first?

Recently I was at a presentation of Angela Duckworth's book **Grit: The Power of Passion and Perseverance** and I was struck by a question from someone in the audience. This lady asked Angela if she was speaking to a young person, would she emphasise developing grit and determination above all else. Angela's reply was that there were many characteristics she would value and that empathy was close to the top of her list.

Research on empathy

In Rosemary Fink's research (2002), her participants seem to have emphasised the feature of empathy. In my own research, many participants said that the experience of finding life tough when they were young, struggling with a world that is not aware of or friendly to dyslexia, had given them a much closer understanding of what it is like to live with disability or other difficulties.

The general concept is that you don't have to have empathy to be successful but that it helps. Recently, Dr Travis Bradberry posted on LinkedIn that successful people keep an open mind; they recognise that they need to practise empathy by putting themselves in other people's shoes.

What is empathy?

So what is empathy? It really is the experience of standing in another person's shoes. Psychologists dissect empathy into 3 slightly different activities:

- First, there's the experience of understanding another person's situation from their perspective, not our own. This is frequently called 'cognitive empathy'.

- Then, there's the sort of empathy where we actually feel someone's pain or distress. As an example of this, if we watch a particularly harrowing film, we might find we empathise so closely with the hurt and pain that we feel distressed ourselves. This 'distress empathy' is not always thought to be healthy as their hurt is not ours, but it can still cause a serious stress reaction in us and it's somewhat contagious, so everyone around us might then feel rather depressed.

- Finally, there's empathetic concern, where we recognise the other person's condition but we are still aware of our own state, of wellbeing for example.

Empathy is not the same as sympathy

Empathy is not the same as sympathy. With sympathy, you reflect another person's situation but from your own viewpoint, not theirs. You might say, 'Yes, I've been there…'

The empathy deficit

In 2006, Barack Obama expressed concern about an 'empathy deficit' because there is a political discussion about whether focusing on ourselves, being independent and self-sufficient, is creating the opposite of empathy. This fosters its own concerns as we are interconnected and self-focus is not good for fostering effective communities.

How empathy is created in the brain

Neurologists have begun to clarify what parts of the brain are involved with our conscious and unconscious thoughts. They also recognise some of the pathways

involved in empathy. The consensus is that we are hard-wired for empathy through 'mirror neurons'.
In MRI examinations, the regions of the brain engaged in emotion and physical sensation light up when you are aware of another's distress. In addition, generosity and altruism also show up in the pleasure centres of the brain. We know that babies are born with a set of expressions designed to stimulate responses from their parents and other carers. Throughout life we use our feelings for communicating and to motivate behaviour. As this allows us to understand the world around us better, it enables us to control our situation and futures better. This would seem to be the genetic advantage behind this hard-wiring.

Tools to assess your own empathy

There are a number of tools to assess empathy, for example the Empathy Quotient which was designed by Simon Baron-Cohen, originally for assessments by mental health practitioners. You can undertake this assessment tool at www.psychology-tools.com/empathy-quotient.

How you can increase your empathy

There are lots of ways that you can increase your empathy if necessary. Here are a few things to try:

- Think about someone close to you. Focus on one of their behaviours. What experiences and shaping do you think forged their views and values and ultimately created their behaviours?

- Watch other people, for example on stations or in airports, and see if you can work out the emotions they have from their facial expression.

- Think about someone you don't like. Can you envision what their situation is that creates their behaviours? It's important to observe and be non-judgemental in this.

- What about widening this out now and thinking about news stories, people from other cultures. What's motivating them? Can you imagine what it's like to stand in their shoes?

- You can role-play empathy. Think about certain potential situations and act out how the person in that situation might be feeling.

Empathy is essentially a state of mind, a way of thinking. Once you have tapped into it, there should be no stopping you.

Empathy's importance in some jobs

Having empathy is very important in certain jobs. It's critical for managing others where you really do need to understand things from your subordinates' perspective in order to get the very best out of them at work. This is the essence of good management. It's also important for collaborative working as it is empathy that builds the necessary trust. In customer relations, it's essential for working out what the customer is feeling and their stance, especially if you are dealing with complaints!

Finally, there is a lot of concern about it within the caring professions. If you research empathy and nursing or medicine, you will find very large amounts of material. In essence, these papers argue that empathetic concern is really important in treating patients. They are more likely to feel listened to; the nurse or doctor will get more, and more relevant, information from the patient; and the health outcomes for patients are higher. However, there isn't much training in empathetic concern within the medical profession training programmes. There is also concern that the empathy shown must include a 'distancing', as distress empathy would make the doctor or nurse more stressed and less able to do their job in the long term.

How to build rapport and listen

We can also focus on learning the elements to empathy, such as building rapport and listening skills. So let's now focus a bit on these.

When we are trying to build rapport, especially with someone we do not know very well, we:

- try to appear non-threatening

- listen carefully to what they have to say and the way that they say it

- use humour to dispel any tension

- watch our own body language and try to exclude any inappropriate signals

- show our empathy with the person

- reflect back common ground that we have established.

In many conversations, you will observe that people often don't listen to each other very carefully – it's an exercise in taking turns to speak. This is not effective for establishing empathy or rapport. What is needed is active listening.

Active listening

In active listening, we put our full attention and concentration on what the other person is saying and their body language. This differentiates it from passive listening, which is really just hearing. We hear things all the time – music in lifts, snatches of conversations, white noise from machines and so on – and you will be aware that this is not like listening. Actively listening to someone is very powerful as it shows that you are focusing on them and that attention is a significant emotional reward. This is where the rapport stems from.

More detailed processes for creating empathy

There are opportunities to look at the psychology of creating empathy in much greater depth. Therefore, I include here a brief introduction to the popular behavioural models of Multiple Intelligences, Emotional Intelligence, Transactional Analysis, and Neuro-Linguistic Programming. These are very big subjects in their own right, though, so I also include some links in case you want to study them in greater detail.

Multiple Intelligences

This is a concept originally developed by Howard Gardner in 1983. He felt that the traditional view of intelligence was much too limited and that we can assess people across 7 different areas. As intelligence is defined as the ability to find ways to succeed when circumstances change, it seems logical that any way of doing that is relevant. The 7 areas are:

- **Visual–Spatial**, which is a commonly recognised ability that some dyslexic adults possess. Some individuals can actually visualise models in 3D, which is extremely useful in areas such as architecture, digital engineering, engineering, and electrical design and installation.

- **Bodily–Kinaesthetic**, which is about the sense of touch and being very aware of the physicality of your body. Aakash Odedra's story in Chapter 6 demonstrates this very well.

- **Musical**, which is about being sensitive to sound and rhythm. Anna Devin's story in Chapter 3 encapsulates this.

- **Interpersonal**, which we would describe here as using empathy. John Levell's story in this chapter demonstrates the strength that this type of intelligence endows.

- **Intrapersonal**, which is about being internally motivated and knowledgeable about how to achieve goals we have set ourselves.

- **Linguistic**, which is about using words effectively. Lord Addington describes how he does this on a daily basis in his story in Chapter 8.

- **Logical–Mathematical**, which is about abstract, conceptual thinking. Many of the respondents in my research spoke about their skills in this area and linked them to spatial awareness.

Gardner went on to draw conclusions that our traditional way of teaching didn't suit everyone and argued for methods which would engage individuals according to their particular type of intelligence. Unsurprisingly, this concept has been popular in dyslexic circles as it does describe a number of the strengths we believe are conferred by dyslexia. We also know that people learn best through multi-sensory methods. If you would like to do an assessment of your intelligences then you can for free at www.literacynet.org/mi/assessment/findyourstrengths.html.

Emotional Intelligence

The model of Emotional Intelligence, measured using Emotional Quotient (E.Q.), became popular after Daniel Goleman published his book on it in 1995. This encapsulated earlier work done on the topic since the 1970s. It has a lot in common with the Multiple Intelligences theory and also argues that only studying I.Q. is too narrow. With the Emotional Quotient there is recognition of the behavioural and personality elements in our social behaviour. We know that having a high I.Q. does not guarantee self-fulfilment or success in life. We also know that people have to have some social grace and understanding of others to succeed. Those who value E.Q. say that, to be successful, you have to have awareness and control of your own emotions and respond to that of others. E.Q. covers 2 types of intelligence:

- Understanding yourself, your goals, intentions, responses and behaviour.

- Understanding others, and their feelings.

This work has evolved, with more behavioural psychologists entering the debate. The focus has shifted onto emotional information processing. In this we perceive emotion, use our emotions to facilitate our thought processes, understand emotions and manage emotions. Individuals with high Emotional Intelligence are effective in social environments; those with less Emotional Intelligence are less effective in social environments. Consequently, there has been considerable interest from work psychologists, H.R. and training managers and their professional institutes in this concept. It is believed that it reduces interpersonal conflict at work (which is very time-consuming and costly for organisations). It is also thought to provide routes to reduce stress for individuals as it teaches people how to manage their responses to others' behaviour. For people professionals, it is used as another way to understand behaviour, management style and future potential.

If you want to find out more about your level of Emotional Intelligence then there is a free test at www.ihhp.com/free-eq-quiz.

Transactional Analysis

Transactional Analysis (T.A.) is a theory developed by Dr Eric Berne in the 1950s. He was working with a group of psychologists who believed that people would be helped significantly in managing their lives if they were aware of a few concepts known to psychologists. They had observed how often communication doesn't work because people are not on the same plane or wavelength as each other. Berne developed T.A. as a means to help everyone learn about effective communication. It's very helpful to use the model as a means to understand where others are coming from. However, it was designed to act as a contractual model, where both parties agree what they want out of the relationship or communication. This requires both parties to be quite specific in the terms of the deal. So within the process of T.A., people are trained to say what it is they want to achieve very clearly and in positive wording. They are also encouraged to include a timeframe and any other specific terms involved. All of this is designed to promote better relationships.

The model hinges on the concept of understanding what state each person is in, and from this what their communication is motivated by and what they may be trying to achieve, often unconsciously. Berne chose to use 3 representations in the model:

- The parent (which represents a state and associated behaviour, of either standards setting or nurturing).

- The adult (which represents the rational, reasoning state and behaviours).

- The child (which represents either the fun-loving, playful state or the sulky irresponsible state and associated behaviours).

Berne's work was substantially developed in 2011 by Mountain Associates, a British consultancy firm specialising in this area. They have more clearly identified the states in which communication takes place effectively and the behaviours which impede it.

Here is an example to demonstrate the basic concept. A dyslexic adult has accepted a new job but did not disclose his dyslexia for fear that he would not be offered the job if he did. He has particular difficulties with personal organisation and time-keeping. At first things go well in the new job and the relationship with his boss is positive and good. Communications between them are centred on the work and are very task-focused and rational.

However, after a while, other pressures mount on the dyslexic adult. The stress of worry is diminishing his life-coping strategies and he is having trouble sleeping because, when he goes to bed, his mind gets more, rather than less, active. This impacts on his ability to get up early enough in the morning to ensure that he has more than enough time to get to work, and use his organisational coping strategies. He begins to be late for work. His boss isn't happy about this and takes him on one side. The boss asks him why he is repeatedly late for work, explaining that this isn't acceptable and says that he wants to agree a way forward with him so that he isn't late anymore (this would be described as being in the 'adult' state). The employee still doesn't want to disclose his dyslexia because now he is even more worried that if he does, he will be considered even less suitable for the job. This means that he cannot discuss his situation entirely openly. Instead, he decides to just go along with the boss and agree to anything to get him out of the room (this would be described as the 'child' state as he isn't thinking about the consequences of his action or taking responsibility for it). They agree that he will be punctual at work for the next 2 months and that this will be monitored.

So the employee manages to get to work on time for the next 2 weeks, but the pressures that cause him to lose sleep are still there and now he's also worried about being late and losing his job. He then is late and the boss asks to see him again. By this stage, the boss has just decided, on the evidence of behaviour available to him, that this employee is just lazy and irresponsible. This time the communication is really tainted between them because there is no openness and now they feel things about each other. You can easily see that this all-too-common problem at work can quickly escalate, with negative communications on both sides and permanent damage to the relationship.

T.A. tries to avoid this happening. It suggests that we can all learn how to operate with each other more effectively by setting up communications and behaving in a way that induces 'adult' state behaviour from both parties. In other words, it's a model that helps us to act empathetically towards each other.

Neuro-Linguistic Programming (N.L.P.)

N.L.P. hails from the 1970s and was created by Richard Bandler, a computer scientist and Gestalt therapist, and Dr John Grinder, a linguist and therapist. It provides an extreme version of understanding where the other person is at, which can be very effective. The aim of N.L.P. is that practitioners can be better aware and in control of themselves, and have better appreciation of others' feelings and behaviour patterns. This increases empathy and improves communication and cooperation. It is more of a philosophy for how to live with general principles to follow and has taken practices from a number of different sources.

N.L.P. is based on 4 operating principles:

- Knowing what outcome you want to achieve.

- Having a clear and sensory understanding of whether you are on the right path to achieve your goal or moving away from it.

- Being sufficiently flexible in your behaviour so you can vary it to achieve your outcome.

- Acting now.

A range of linguistic patterns and behaviours are used by its practitioners to help others change their beliefs and behaviours. Throughout, practitioners monitor the other person they are interacting with and change their behaviour to help secure the desired outcome. This sounds rather patronising described like this, but in practice that is not the case. The underlying principles which guide this model include things such as having respect for others and their beliefs, recognising that the way you interpret the world may not be the same as others' interpretation, and that no one person's view is necessarily right. Crucially in terms of empathy, N.L.P. teaches that when you communicate with others, the message they receive is based on their interpretation of what you have said, done and the state you are in. When you use the tools from N.L.P., 2-way communication is enhanced and this is very useful for creating a higher state of empathy.

Links for more about these concepts

The descriptions above are a very brief introduction. Training to be a T.A. or N.L.P. practitioner takes years, so inevitably here I have barely touched the surface. Therefore, if you want to look into this in greater detail then here are some links:

- For Multiple Intelligences, Gardner and Howard's work, see: www.danielgoleman.info/howard-gardner-multiple-intelligences.

- For Emotional Intelligence, see: www.danielgoleman.info/topics/emotional-intelligence.

- For Transactional Analysis, see: www.ericberne.com/transactional-analysis.

- For N.L.P., see: www.nlpacademy.co.uk/what_is_nlp.

Case study: John Levell

John Levell works for Ernst & Young, as an Associate Partner. He is a founder and sponsor of their Dyslexia Network and a current Trustee of the British Dyslexia Association.

John is an excellent strategic thinker and a hugely empathetic individual. When you talk with him, you feel you are the only person he has focus for. He is also able to take in and reflect back to you all the facts, and provide new insight as well as the emotions implicit in any situation. This, combined with his strength in strategic thinking, enables him to weigh up complex problems, including all the human elements, and suggest ways forward that cover all angles. This is apparent from the story of his career.

John was an only child with a very supportive mother and stepfather – both of whom worked in education and supported him in different ways. He exhibited learning difficulties through his early attainment in a number of subjects. However, good teaching, the support of his parents, additional private tuition and a substantial amount of hard work meant that he overcame initial difficulties and gained exceptionally good results in national exams at age 16.

Despite early difficulties, his self-image was that of a highly capable person – but questions had already begun to arise as to why he seemed to have unpredictable outcomes.

He went on to study for 4 Advanced levels, in maths, physics, music and music performance history. This is when things went awry. Whilst gaining some of these qualifications he didn't get the grades needed to go to the 'redbrick' universities of his choice – so looked for a job that would take him towards his chosen career. The job was in a recording studio making the tea! He initially worked shifts of 7 days, 12 hours a day, and then one day off. To learn the about the industry he stayed on longer at night than others to get access to the technology.

John was then recommended by this employer for a job at George Martin's studio in London, as an assistant recording engineer – the industry was changing towards digital formats and John was someone who already understood this technology. Here was our first example of John's strengths in strategy and empathy, in this case developing an empathic relationship with his boss. It's not often that an employer will find a better job for the tea boy!

At George Martin's studio he worked as assistant engineer with artists such as Robert Plant, Bryan Adams and Bryan Ferry. However, despite early success, John was finding the world a confusing and difficult place to navigate. He left to go freelance and then made what he now describes as an 'accidental career change', in a gap between music industry work, to a job with I.T. content with his mother's accountants.

John's early career became a patchwork quilt of new jobs, mainly gained through recommendation based on outstanding work – because he is highly empathetic, tenacious and also sees problems differently.

Having taken an accidental turn to a more conventional career, he decided to address the perceived impact of his lack of a university education. He began studying for a range of qualifications, ending in an M.B.A., and succeeded with distinctions in the coursework but found the exam process very challenging.

Now with an apparently more conventional C.V., after a number of years owning his own business, he took a job at Deloitte, building a new business within this large firm. It was very successful and allowed him to progress rapidly through the firm – as far as the partner admissions process.

Almost simultaneously, he failed the partner admissions process and his oldest son was diagnosed with dyslexia. Shortly after, at age 42, John was diagnosed with dyslexia himself and suddenly had a new insight. He understood the cause of the gap between his own self-image and his experience of life. The unpredictable journey, characterised by a combination of highs (where he had achieved things others had felt were not possible) and lows (where the most basic skills suddenly let him down) became predictable – and he could take steps to mitigate weaknesses and focus on strengths.

The revelation was so significant that he decided on a change of direction and moved organisations, joining Ernst & Young (E.Y.) to be a part of building their consulting practice. In 2008, with a number of colleagues at E.Y., he decided to do something to support other dyslexics within the firm and set up the E.Y. Dyslexia Network.

There is no doubt that many organisations, including professional and city firms, still have very low rates of disclosure of dyslexia. However, within E.Y. this is beginning to change as, thanks to the work of John and his colleagues, there is a functioning 'help-desk' run by volunteers within the E.Y. Network. There is an annual conference event with external speakers and opportunities for those interested in dyslexia to mingle and chat. The Network is also listed as a support group on the company's website and seen as part of their inclusivity that enables them to recruit more talented people. There's a mentoring scheme, and training is offered within the main company training menu for coping strategies for dyslexic employees. Disclosure is still an issue, as it is in most employment situations, but partly thanks to John's persistence and empathy, a significant journey has been travelled, which is now used as an example for other firms to emulate.

For the future, he believes that one of the major untapped opportunities, particularly for larger employers, is to actively harness the creativity and diversity of thought present in its neuro-diverse people to fuel innovation and drive change.

Key points from this chapter

★ Empathy may not be critical to success in all areas of life but it really is paramount in some.

★ The most effective form of empathy is where you understand someone's situation and feelings but you do not get drawn in to own these; you remain within your own state of being.

★ You can use an online tool to assess your level of empathy.

★ There are several activities that you can engage in to grow your capacity for empathy.

★ There is a lot of research on empathy for roles in healthcare where it has been proved to improve patient health.

★ Empathy is a key component of establishing rapport, and that is important in many job roles.

★ You can learn more about establishing empathy from the concepts of Multiple Intelligences, Emotional Intelligence, Transactional Analysis and Neuro-Linguistic Programming.

Chapter 8

You Need to Use Your Verbal Influencing Skills

*'Political chaos is connected with the decay of language...
one can probably bring about some improvement by
starting at the verbal end.'*

George Orwell

Gaining understanding

Having good verbal skills may, in part, be due to finding
writing more difficult. Because dyslexic children prefer
to talk rather than write, they develop their talking skills
even more than their peers. However, the research shows
that successful dyslexic people tend to be good verbally
and at story-telling. They use metaphor and stories so
that others understand not just the facts but also engage
emotionally with the pitch. Here is an example of the use

of metaphor like this: 'Dyslexic adults are everywhere, hidden in the bedrock of our society. Like diamonds, they may need a little polish for the areas that are weaker but then we can see their brilliance shine out.'

Influencing others

In life and work, you cannot achieve huge change on your own. This is very obvious if we look at the vast numbers of people involved in successful campaigns, especially those achieved through social media. One voice on Twitter will not cut it, but persuading many to join in can change the world. To bring this down to a more imaginable scale, if you are managing a team of people, they will all have their own views and motivations. The skill of the effective manager is to influence those individuals so they will follow a particular strategy or plan. So, it is clear that the art of persuasion and influencing is a very valuable commodity to have. It is definitely a requirement in management, politics, sales and marketing – and an essential skill for parenting!

Influencing covers both persuading others and, sometimes, negotiation. These skills are not too difficult to learn or to improve upon.

How to be persuasive

First we will look at persuasion. This is the skill of persuading others to convince others to follow your lead without significant change to your concept.

Step 1

Create a strong argument for why others should do what you suggest. This means developing your lines of argument, all the points that are benefits for why others should agree with you. You could use a concept map to develop these ideas.

Step 2

Work out what the objections might be to your concept. You may need to think of ways of reducing these objections or avoiding them in your plan.

Step 3

Consider what might be the emotional pull to your concept. Dyslexic individuals can be very good at communicating emotional contexts through metaphor and story. If you give people both a rational argument and the emotional pull, you have the strongest case possible.

Step 4

Communicate your concept to others, but focus your attention on them. This means actively listening to them, finding out what their views and expectations are, showing them respect and presenting your points calmly and in positive language.

We can see this in action in the following example.

Example of persuasion in action

Smoking is acknowledged to damage people's health. The use of campaigns to persuade people, particularly young people, to disengage from smoking is widespread in many countries. Behind these public health campaigns are lots of research projects to identify the facts. So, for example, in Australia generally the numbers of young people smoking reduced after a government campaign. However, there was particular concern about young indigenous females where the numbers did not shrink. The research indicated that smoking was a cultural norm and that they needed to smoke to be part of the adult social group. The research recommended that the facts on health outcomes be given to older indigenous women so they would then be persuaded to influence the younger women to change their attitudes to smoking.

Similarly in Canada, there was also concern about young women smoking and that the numbers were rising rather than levelling out as in other demographic groups. The research also found that young women's reason for starting to smoke was social, to fit in.

So, not only did the argument need to include rational reasons for not starting to smoke or to quit smoking, it also had to take account of emotional social factors. Only by doing both were these campaigns likely to succeed.

Force-field analysis

If in the course of listing objections to your concept you find there are rather a lot of these, you may want to use force-field analysis to plan how to strengthen your case. This analysis is also very useful in planning to negotiate, which we will be thinking about next.

The aim is to work out the forces for your concept and the forces against it. All you have to do is create a list of all the things that will push your concept forward and then all the things that will hinder it. You then give each one a number or weighting out of 10. There is nothing scientific about this, just ascribe a strength to each item according to your own opinion. After you have done this, add up the numbers in the 'forces for' column, and also those in the 'forces against' column. If the number for the 'forces for' exceeds the number for the 'forces against', then it is likely that your argument will win. However, if the cumulative forces against are stronger, it will probably fail. You can then work out which forces need strengthening or which need to be weakened to increase your chance of success.

Negotiating skills

Negotiating occurs where 2 or more parties come together to reach agreement on a way forward. This is likely to involve some concessions by each party. There are, however, pitfalls to negotiation. If one party decides to win at all costs then they may succeed, but only in the short term as the other party will avoid working with them again. There is also a saying that 'a compromise means no one has succeeded'. If the compromises made are really radical, there is a danger that the original aim for the negotiation and desire to seek a solution is completely lost. So here is an approach for successful negotiation.

Step 1
Carefully identify the overall aim.

Step 2
Listen very closely to the other party, both for their aims and the climate in which they are operating. This is about using empathy, another key skill that many dyslexic individuals have.

Step 3
Identify all the issues in conjunction with the other party and then identify common ground.

Step 4
Agree the process by which you will negotiate and by when you want to have concluded the negotiation.

Step 5
Work out what you can concede that will not defeat the overall aim. Then discuss problem areas with the other party and make suitable compromises.

Step 6

Once agreement has been reached, it needs to be written down and each party needs to study it to make sure that there are no issues of non-agreement. Then you are ready to communicate your outcomes more widely.

We can see that both direct persuasion and negotiating are used in influencing others. We can see this in action in the case study for this chapter on Lord Addington, a British politician.

Making presentations

One of the key ways in which we use our verbal influencing skills at work is when we are making presentations. This often terrifies adults with dyslexia as they fear that all their challenges will be exposed. However, there are good coping strategies that can be learned which virtually ensure success. Here is the process to make effective presentations and the coping strategies at each stage.

Preparation is key to successful presenting

There is a very famous and accurate saying by Benjamin Franklin: 'By failing to prepare, you are preparing to fail.' This is entirely true when it comes to making speeches or giving presentations. So our first step is the preparation.

How to prepare

You prepare by working on the topic and any research needed; the time allocated for the presentation; information about the audience; the outcomes you want; and logistics such as the journey and the venue. So let's look at each of these in detail.

Researching the topic

The topic may be something you have suggested or may be given to you by somebody else. Either way, you are going to need to research it thoroughly and that takes time. Allow yourself more time than you think is necessary because it will probably take longer than you estimate. This is a really critical phase because if you are completely comfortable with your topic, you will feel confident and less threatened on the day. This is important because it will reduce the stress that might impact upon your coping strategies.

You can use your normal coping strategies for dealing with written material when doing the research. Everything that is available on the computer can be heard using text-to-speech software. If you don't own any, then there are free versions available. Amongst the best are Natural Reader (www.naturalreaders.com), Ivona, which has different voices to choose from (www.ivona.com), Audio Book Maker (http://audiobookmaker.com) and Zabaware (www.zabaware.com/reader). Your computer may well already have a text-to-speech facility in the Settings section. If the material is in books, then you can scan the pages, upload them to your computer and again use the software to hear rather than read these pages.

The next stage is to go through the material and select what you need. A good way to do this is to copy and paste what you need onto a blank document on your computer. You can then read or listen to it, and colour-code the sections you find that are the ones you want. After this you can create a concept map to organise the material. As a reminder on how to do this, use a large piece of paper and put the theme for your talk in the centre. Then add items that you want to include around this with lines (strong ones for important connections) out to the items or between items. You can use specialist software such as Inspiration (www.inspiration.com) to do this. There are also lots of free concept mapping programs such as Mind Maple (www.mindmaple.com) and Lucid chart (www.lucidchart.com), which is particularly good for developing charts and diagrams that you might want to include in your talk. You can organise your topics by numbering the different items on your concept map.

Time allotted

The amount of time you are given will limit the scope of your presentation. Bear in mind that you will always take longer to present than you initially think. (See more on this in the section on planning the content, below.) Once you have written your talk, you must practise it several times out loud so that you can get used to the flow of it and also work out how long it takes.

Your audience
The more you can find out about the audience, the better. This will enable you to pitch your talk appropriately. It's useful to think about their existing knowledge of the topic, their ages (for example, it's very different presenting to children compared with adults, and young adults generally have a shorter attention span and need more activity). Can you also find out what else they are going to be listening to during the day?

Outcomes you want
If it's a technical presentation, you may want to ensure that you get some specific information across to your audience. You will need to prepare for how this will happen. You can usually do this by repetition and engaging all their senses.

Logistics
In order to reduce the stress on the day as much as possible, try to find out all you can about the venue and the journey there. Travelling and finding your way to places can be one of the key stressors for dyslexic adults. The reason for this is that it uses up a lot of working memory to hold information about timetables and locations and you are usually trying to do this within a short, set timeframe. So by making it as easy as possible you can reduce the loading on your working memory and keep the stress low.

A good coping strategy is to have all the key information you need for getting there on one sheet of paper which you can find easily. You can colour-code different parts of it; for example, the times of trains and buses could be in one colour and the address in another.

You can print instructions on how to find places using programs such as Google maps and Bing, while CityMapper is a good app for journey planning though currently it only covers a limited number of cities. Making a note of visual clues about the venue can be really helpful too.

Knowing where to find the room on the day, and what is the timetable for the presentations, is all necessary preparation.

Plan your clothes for the day. Make sure they are comfortable – you do not want to have pinching shoes, or too tight a collar or waistband. Not only will that make you feel uncomfortable, it will show in your face!

How to plan the content of your presentation

You will need to decide what the core points that you want to get across are. If you are speaking for 10 minutes, 4 key points are quite enough. You can plan these 4 points, and a fifth if you wish, which can be left out but is comforting to have available. Generally, the best way to do this is with a P.E.P. structure: Point, Example, Point. If you plan your talk that way, you can always add in or extract a P.E.P. according to how the time goes.

Think of your whole talk as being like a meal. You need an interesting starter to whet the audience's appetite, then comes the main course (your 4 P.E.P. points), and finally you want to finish with something tasty.

It is crucial that your talk is dyslexia-friendly for those in your audience that are dyslexic (and there will be 1 in 7 with dyslexia or a related condition). However, everyone, whether they are dyslexic or not, learns best and remembers presentations made this way. Next we look at how to make it dyslexia-friendly.

Dyslexic people tend to be global learners – they need to see the overview so they can use their comprehension skills to pick up the details. So the first thing to do, other than welcoming the audience and if necessary introducing yourself, is to set the scene and give an overview. You need to tell them what you are going to tell them and how you intend to do so.

Most people with dyslexia have at least one sense that is weaker, so this needs to be planned for. Use visual, auditory and kinaesthetic methods to make your points. For example, you might put up a PowerPoint slide, talk about it and then pass around something to touch, such as a sample related to the talk or a short handout. If you can add in something which engages with the audience's feelings then you will have covered all the bases. This could be something humorous, controversial, sad, happy, or anything that arouses passion. The connections with the senses and emotions will also work for you as a presenter as you will remember the items you need to present even better if they are attached to feelings.

Where you are using PowerPoint slides, remember to make the print big (preferably font size 20 or above).

Use a sans serif font such as Arial or Verdana. Add pictures if you can, instead of relying only on words. Use initial capitals and lower case, and don't underline words. The background to your slides needs to be a pastel colour instead of white (a creamy yellow is best) for those with a visual distraction (which occurs with half the people with dyslexia).

Most dyslexic adults worry that they will lose the plot of their presentation. This rarely happens in practice because you will get a spurt of adrenalin as you start and that speeds up your responses. Often the flow of your presentation will be committed to long-term memory by the time you have practised the talk in advance. Long-term memory is not affected for those with dyslexia so this is a helpful coping mechanism. In addition, we remember by association so if the ideas flow from one to another in a clear sequence, the audience will follow you better and it will act as a memory jogger to you too.

You can use flash cards for your talk. These should be small enough for you to hold in one hand. Number them at the top left-hand side, then punch a hole in the top right-hand side. Now you can feed a tag through the holes, so that they are kept in sequence. This will avoid any danger of you dropping them and getting them out of order, avoiding another nightmare thought! You can put your timings on these so you can keep track of where you are as you present. Finally, it is possible to take the full script with you, but try very hard not to be tempted to read from it as that will damage your skill at presenting.

Nonetheless, it can act as a good comfort blanket to know that you have it should anything unforeseen happen.

How to deliver your presentation

Smile at the audience as soon as you start. This will help establish rapport with them and also make you look confident. Everyone feels nervous giving presentations until they have had a lot of experience; just accept it, it's normal. However, the way to deal with those nerves is to make sure they don't get out of hand. We do this by reducing risks and threats. You can see now why I have stressed the role of preparation – it takes out many of the worries. The audience are on your side and want you to be a success, they are rooting for you.

If you are standing in front of the audience, then take control of the space. It's just space, not scary, and it's your space for now. Stand up straight so that you can breathe easily and take a few deep breaths as you approach the spot where you will begin. Now here's a trick: before you go out and are visible to the audience, tip your head down to your knees. You will get a rush of blood to the head and that will help your brain work well.

When you speak, talk as if it were to an individual in the audience. Make it personal. Imagine that the person is sitting towards the back wall and you will naturally project your voice.

Finally, slow down. When you are presenting, the audience wants to keep up with what you are saying and have time to process it. That requires us to speak more slowly than in everyday speech. If you keep an eye on the timings on your flash cards, that will help you slow down, as the natural inclination is to speed up as you go along.

At the end, remind them of what you were talking about and thank them for attending. You can now relax and will probably have surprised yourself by how well it has gone.

Case study: Lord Addington

Lord Addington, 6th Baron, entered the U.K. House of Lords at the age of 22 on 1 July 1986, after taking his father's title and becoming the youngest serving peer. After graduating from the University of Aberdeen, he became an active member of the Lords. He took the position of sports spokesman in 1993, has also been the spokesman for the Liberal Democrats on Defence, the Environment and Education and spent 11 years in the Whips' Office, 7 of which were as Deputy Chief Whip.

He played first-class rugby in his youth and is also Vice-President of the U.K. Sports Association. He is captain of the Commons and Lords Rugby and Football teams, and played in many Parliamentary World Cup competitions. He was on the organising committee for the 2016 tournament in England before the World Cup. He currently plays for his local Old Boys' club. Lord Addington also competes in the Parliament's pancake race every year. He is a veteran of the Commons versus Lords 'Total War' rugby matches and is the only person still taking part who was in the initial competition in 1987!

Having dyslexia has encouraged him to lend his support to the British Dyslexia Association (B.D.A.); he was active as a Vice-President for many years, and was appointed as their President in 2015. He is also Chair of Microlink, an assistive technology company. Lord Addington has campaigned tirelessly over the last 30 years for those with disabilities, especially dyslexia and related conditions. 'Being dyslexic, I don't write my speeches, but I do like to know what I am talking about so I do quite a lot of research for them.' His work is to influence using verbal persuasion skills.

He has been successful in this, keeping dyslexia in the spotlight and raising questions in the House of Lords whenever the government's policy changes for the worse for dyslexics. In recent years, he achieved a very significant change to apprenticeships. Apprentices, where we see a higher proportion of those with dyslexia, are now entitled to reasonable adjustments in their core skill tests and this is being rolled out across the U.K. More recently, he has been campaigning with the B.D.A. for dyslexia awareness to be included in initial teacher training in the U.K. On 9 June 2016, he presented the first steps of a Bill to influence change in Initial Teacher Training. The purpose of the Bill is to enable all teachers to start to fulfil their legal duty and to be able to recognise Specific Learning Difficulties, and to be able to educate all children.

Lord Addington has passion and purpose, and clearly is an exemplar for verbal influencing skills, as was remarked upon by another member of the House of Lords, Lord Storey: 'My Lords, I start by thanking my noble friend Lord Addington for securing this debate. His tenacity and perspicacity in this area knows no bounds.'

Key points from this chapter

★ Influencing others can include both rational lines of argument and an emotional interaction with others.

★ Story-telling and metaphor are excellent ways of creating emotional understanding and empathy.

★ There are step-by-step processes for both persuasion and negotiation which can readily be learned.

★ Influencing is a combination of persuasion and negotiation.

★ Presenting is a necessary skill in most jobs, and by making your talk dyslexia-friendly you will help the audience and yourself.

Chapter 9

You Need to Make Effective, Fluent Use of Coping Strategies

'By adulthood, many people are able to compensate through technology, reliance on others and an array of self help mechanisms.'

British Dyslexia Association

We need coping strategies to get around the difficult bits

Whilst our wonderful and different brains give us all sorts of strengths, unfortunately these same differences can also lead to challenges. It is well understood in the research that those with dyslexia will continue to have issues with literacy throughout their lives. It doesn't mean that you can't operate quite well, it just means that you probably won't be as fast at comprehending what you are reading as someone without dyslexia. Similarly, someone with mild Asperger's Syndrome may well be extremely good at focusing on and completing numerical tasks but they still won't be a natural at interpreting facial expressions. However, this is not the end of the world – we now have vast opportunities to use coping strategies to surmount most of our issues.

Developing your own coping strategies

We saw the stress that our respondents put on this in their answers to the questionnaire. One of the things that dyslexic individuals can do is problem solve. Most dyslexic people are good at solving their own problems. From an early age they find ways around their problems. They create coping strategies. I was diagnosed with profound dyscalculia only a few years ago. Of course, I knew that I had had problems with remembering how to work out fractions and percentages from my school days, but I hadn't even heard of dyscalculia until about 10 years ago. Anyway, one of the things I remember from the assessment process was the psychologist commenting on just how many coping strategies I had developed. She said she had never seen so many different ways of approaching a number problem!

Some common coping strategies people have developed

Examples of people using coping strategies that they have developed include watching films or listening to music rather than reading books on holiday; making phone calls rather than sending emails or texts; and coping with spelling by getting their partner to proofread their work. Creating effective coping strategies for yourself is really positive, and because our challenges are often specific to ourselves, it's important too as there may not be a readymade, off-the-shelf solution for us. However, it is worth reflecting on these strategies to make sure they are all positive for us. We don't want to cut ourselves off from experiences because our strategy is avoidance.

Fluency is key

The key to effectively using coping strategies is that they must become fluent. We need them to be really embedded. Specialists talk about 'automaticity' and what they mean is that the person can carry out the activity whilst being engaged on something else. So, for example, you can drive a car with all the actions appearing to be automatic and still carry on a conversation with your passenger. As a successful adult, we really need to be able to be as fluent and automatic using our text-to-speech software as a fluent reader is reading a book.

You have to practise using coping strategies

There is no short-cut to achieving fluency with our coping strategies. The only way we will achieve this is through considerable practice through use. There are lots of arguments about how long you need to practise to develop a skill, but there is no argument that it is a lot of hours.

Coping strategies go when we are stressed

The other thing to note about coping strategies is that we tend to lose them when we are really stressed. So, we go for a job interview, have it all planned out, but once the adrenalin gets going then our usual coping mechanisms go too.

Funding for software and support

Funding for software or support can be a very big issue. In the U.K. and Australia, the governments have schemes for employees to receive some funding towards the purchase of reasonable adjustments, though the uptake is not huge. Some large employers will provide adjustments, and in some cases suitable software programs are installed on their networks as they have been found to help efficiency for staff who are not dyslexic too! The increasing numbers of free apps and tools on the internet is extremely useful if you are self-funding.

So now let's take a tour of the most typical coping strategies we can use.

Assistive technology

Reading

Text readers are probably the most commonly recommended reasonable adjustment. They have come a long way from the initial programs. However, work is still on going to improve the range of synthetic voices available on them. They are also now available as free apps for phones and have been included as standard in e-readers such as the Kindle. This is particularly helpful in the workplace context as you can download professional texts, some professional journals and newspapers onto e-readers.

In addition to the choice of voice for the individual, care has to be taken in recommending a specific product if the individual has another impairment, such as a hearing impairment. Some products work better with hearing aids, for example, than others.

If the individual's job requires a lot of form-filling, then there is specific software available to support this.

For the individual with a visual distraction or anyone where the glare of black print on a white background causes difficulty reading, there are programs which change the background colour. It is also possible to have a reading ruler on-screen which helps the person keep focus on the line or section that they are reading. Coloured filters are also available to fit over the entire computer screen, and coloured overlays are also used with books and printed text to reduce glare.

One of the things individuals will need to be encouraged to do is to request documents whenever possible in a digital format so that they can use their text reader on them. It is possible to scan printed documents into the computer, but this is time-consuming and the product is not always perfect where the original is handwritten, for example. A variety of scanners, including scanning pens, are available.

Typing and writing

The amount of handwriting we all do is decreasing and it is estimated that, in 5 years' time, many of us will not write at all! This is also good news for dyslexic individuals who may still have residual problems with either the legibility of their handwriting or the automaticity of accurate spelling.

It is generally a good idea for anyone to be able to touch-type and there are specific software programs for those with dyslexia to use to learn this skill. These reinforce reading and spelling and are by their very nature multi-sensory and repetitive, so are well designed for the dyslexic learner.

Generating new ideas is not a problem for most dyslexic individuals, but capturing them in text might be! There are many concept-mapping software programs which are very useful for this. The more useful programs offer an opportunity for the content to be shown as a linear document as well, and this can be really useful for the individual who has a report or long document to plan and develop.

Word-processing packages have good facilities within them for spell-checking. There are also products for grammar-checking which work reasonably well and electronic dictionaries can be helpful too. Using a text reader to read out what you have written can also be a good way of spotting the inadvertent error. It is more difficult to get around the issue of simply not spotting that you have made a mistake or used another word than the one you intended. Sometimes being trained to read a document backwards (which has to be done manually) will help you spot it, but for documents going to an external audience you may still feel you want it proofread by someone else. It is quite strange that you can go back to a document 2 days later and spot something, and you really cannot understand the trick your brain played on you previously and why something has got into your writing that you did not intend. Trading tasks with other colleagues and asking for proofreading is pretty standard in most organisations so those with dyslexia should not be shy in asking for this adjustment by their colleagues.

Voice recognition software is useful for those who cannot type, especially if they have another condition such as a bad back. These still require the individual to teach the software to recognise their voice, though the time this takes has now been drastically reduced, in some cases to about 20 minutes of reading aloud. The individual will need to learn the commands within the program and how to make best use of it. It will still take the user some time to become really proficient with this software but the investment in time can be very worthwhile, especially for the most seriously dyslexic person.

Organising yourself

Whilst most people think of dyslexia as being an issue with reading and spelling, they are much less aware of the impact of a weaker working memory – which is extremely common with all specific learning difficulties. If you can't hold more than 2 or 3 things in your head at once and manipulate these ideas, then it makes life much trickier. Working life has become faster paced with the development of email, the internet, social networking and texting. Keeping up with all this communication and the need to organise it is demanding.

Fortunately, there are good programs for organising and confirming appointments and for creating and managing to-do lists. B.D.A. has a free app, BDADysplay, which teaches time management and organisational principles, through the medium of games. It is available through the iTunes store.

Managing meetings

The combination of text readers to get up to speed ahead of time on agendas and meetings' papers, as well as software for organising meetings and setting alarms so you are reminded to go, all provide good support in advance of a meeting. Many dyslexic employees state that meetings, especially those with lots of pre-reading and reports, or those with an emotional bias such as interviews or appraisal meetings, are the things that cause them most stress in the workplace. Meetings tend to put a lot of pressure on working memory as there are things to remember from the reports and potentially a lot of people are contributing their ideas. The dyslexic person wants to be able to process all this information and also have space to come up with their own contributions.

One of the things that can help with this overload is to record the meeting. There are good digital recorders designed for this purpose, but they usually work only in combination with voice-activated software. They are compatible with most word-processing programs so that personal notes, though not the whole meeting, can be automatically typed up subsequently.

Software training

It is essential that adequate training in using the recommended software is given. Workplace needs assessors often talk about individuals they have seen who have been provided with assistive software 5 years previously but it is unused because they have not realised that they needed sufficient training to be able to become automatic in its use. Working with software involves integrating new ways of working, and this is a change in behaviour which can easily take up to 6 months to implement. However, if the individual does receive effective software training and is prepared to stick at it, the results can be life-changing.

Individual and personal strategies

Working memory strategies

There are lots of ways in which you can generate ideas that will help you cope with the things you find difficult. Let's take a few examples.

Splitting numbers

Most people with dyslexia and related Sp.L.D.s seem to have trouble with their working memory. This is the part of the short-term memory system where you hold an idea in your head and manipulate it. So, for example, if we are trying to do a simple sum, we need to hold the 2 numbers in our head, and then remember how to add them together, and then hold the product in our head. This is working memory in action. So, if our working memory is weaker than typical, we can use many ways to support it. We can create lists so we don't rely on our memory; if we're doing that sum, we can write down the 2 numbers so we don't have to remember them. Alternatively, we can record our lists on our mobile phones so we don't have to write anything down.

Using routines

We can also use routines so that we are not stressing our memory. The routine will enable us to act on autopilot so that we can keep our precious memory for the unpredictable items.

Scaffolding

We can use 'scaffolding' to help our memories. A good example of this is where you have a standard grocery list and then just add new items to it. Most online shopping stores offer you the chance to work with your previously bought items, and that can become your scaffold – you don't have to remember everything.

Breaking tasks down

We can break tasks down. If your problem is that you can only remember 2 numbers of the 4 needed for your bank P.I.N. number, then one way forward is to use the same 2 numbers repeated. Or you could use muscle memory instead of your short-term memory so you learn over time the pattern of the buttons you need to press and where they are, and you can then do it without referring to the numbers at all.

Locus method

You can take the idea or position or location further. If you need to remember something, put it somewhere particular and then remember where it was and you may be able access it more easily.

Mnemonics

Mnemonics are aids we all use to remember things. They usually take the first letter of the items and then a silly phrase is made up using those letters. For example, if you want to remember how to spell 'beautiful' you can learn the phrase '**b**ig **e**lephants **a**re **u**gly' and you have the difficult spelling pattern sorted out. A more adult version might be how to remember the number of 'c's and 's's in 'necessary' with the mnemonic 'condoms for safe sex'! Here is a mnemonic for you to remember our 10 characteristics of successful dyslexic adults. Each initial letter is the beginning of the characteristic, such as D for determination, which gives us a silly sentence to prompt our memory: 'Dyslexic adults can succeed, nurture excellent ideas conquering many problems.'

Determination

Atypical problem-solving skills

Coping strategies

Self-esteem

Niche

Empathy

Influencing skills

Creativity

Mentors

Passion

Visual clues work for some people. So, in trying to learn people's names, you might associate their name with a visual prompt, perhaps a picture of something, and the association will help you recall their name.

It is also possible to use kinaesthetic prompts, such as counting things off on your fingers. For example, perhaps we want to remember the 5 objections to our argument, so we count each off against a finger; and returning later to our fingers will help us remember them.

These are just examples of personal prompts to support our working memory so you can imagine that the opportunities for coping strategies to support our individual challenges are immense. Whilst a dyslexia specialist will know many coping strategies, if you can't access that sort of support, a good way of discovering them is to work with a friend. You can describe the challenge you have and then they can help you come up with solutions.

Someone to help you

There are a few things that we may find just impossible to learn to do and there aren't obvious coping strategies to support that activity. In working with adults with dyslexia and Sp.L.D.s over many years, I have frequently heard how their partners support them. Many managers take work home overnight and get their partners to proofread it for them, ready for the next day. Many individuals are assisted with organising themselves and diary management. Others, particularly those affected by dyscalculia or dyspraxia, are supported by their partners producing maps and instructions for them to navigate by.

Case study: Neil Cottrell

Neil Cottrell is C.E.O. of LexAble, a company that he set up and which develops intelligent, automatic spelling correction software.

Neil was 10 years old when he was diagnosed as being dyslexic. He believes that a combination of being recognised as a child who put in effort and tried to please the teachers, combined with a stark contrast between his achievements in most subjects except reading and spelling, led to a sympathetic approach by his teachers. His parents were extremely supportive and researched dyslexia and what could be done about his challenges, and bought him his first notebook computer.

After his diagnosis, he was statemented and spent an hour a week having specialist support and then, in preparation for secondary school, he started using a computer. He was able to word-process on his computer and he started to use assistive technology. He says that using text-to-speech software was a game-changer for him. He also started to use concept mapping software. Things were good at secondary school and he was not bullied, despite his different approach to study. As an example of teacher support, he describes how the school requested a reader for exams and the exam board refused but his parents and the deputy head fought back, the latter threatening to take the exam board to the Court of Human Rights!

Neil rather underplays his talents, and one of these from an early age was clearly empathy. He describes how despite not being very confident then, he would speak to all teachers new to him and explain how he worked and what he needed. The issues of working memory had not been explained to him with his diagnosis of dyslexia. As is common for dyslexic children, the complexities of secondary school require more personal organisation and loading on memory. He found remembering dates connected to arbitrary historical events particularly difficult to master, and also had difficulty organising himself with the right resources for lessons. So he got a small notebook and put the timetable into the back of it with a list of what he needed for each lesson. 'I started outsourcing my memory early on.' This made him more organised than many of the other pupils who relied on their memory. He used his laptop in all lessons and it worked pretty well.

When he was about 15, he hated the red lines appearing on his typing and the constant spell-checking he had to do. So he learned a bit about computer programming via online tutorials. Then he put together a program for autocorrecting his work. Neil found that he really liked writing software so he kept on improving his program as a hobby. He got 3 A levels in Physics, Maths and P.E., and scored grade 'A' in all of them.

He applied to do a degree in Psychology. He had done work experience with a clinical psychologist and his mother was also a clinical psychologist. He also had some experience working with children with special educational needs. So his first thought as a career was to become a clinical psychologist. However, tales of stretched resources, and having to focus on cost management in the N.H.S., made him think that he wanted to build something less fettered, with the opportunity for more growth. He really enjoyed his time at Cardiff University. By then he had good adjustments so rarely had serious problems. Again, he made the staff aware of what he needed. He spent a lot of time scanning in books so that he could hear rather than read the texts. Later in his studies, there was more focus on journals, and as they are available online he was able to use text-to-speech software directly on them. He got the top marks in the year in his degree exams and the award for the best dissertation.

After his degree, he anticipated joining a graduate development scheme at a large company. However, he went to see the people involved in Student Enterprise at the university to see how he could get his autocorrect software out to help other students with needs like him. They persuaded him that there was significant market potential in this product and unless he gave this some full-time commitment, then he wouldn't be able to reach the sizable group of people he wanted to help. So, Neil set up his company, LexAble, and started to talk to the needs assessors under the Disabled Student Allowance (D.S.A.) scheme. However, he didn't feel very comfortable being 'out there' and preferred to spend time in his room, doing development work on his software program.

Consequently, 9 months after starting up, he wasn't making any money and had begun to think of giving up and getting that corporate job. Fortunately, at this time, the B.D.A. had set up a mentoring scheme and Neil was introduced to someone who was an experienced entrepreneur, having set up his own successful web design company during the dotcom revolution. He saw the potential for Neil's company and rebuilt Neil's confidence about how big a difference this product could make to others. So Neil dropped everything else, went out and talked to needs assessors and set his own target for the next 6 months' sales figures. He hit the target and saw that success was possible.

LexAble is now a successful company based in Cardiff with their major product, Global Autocorrect. He now has staff to do software development and he says that the company doesn't take up all his time. Neil has become a voluntary 'Entrepreneur in Residence' at Cardiff University. Through this he is now mentoring other people with ideas and business start-ups. He loves these chats as the individuals are interesting, passionate and committed to action. Neil can intuitively see the jigsaw puzzle in enterprises and home in on the key things to focus upon.

Neil exemplifies so much of what this book is about. He is a success and he describes how he is really, really enjoying life at the moment as he has a young family and this life model gives him the flexibility to spend time with them, which is important to him.

Key points from this chapter

★ We need to use coping strategies to get around our difficulties.

★ There will always be some residual issues on literacy for dyslexic adults.

★ You can and will have developed your own coping strategies.

★ There is an abundance of assistive technology available, and quite a lot now is apps which are cheap or free.

★ Human support is very valuable.

Chapter 10

Family and Mentors' Assistance Really Matters

'Do not train a child to learn by force or hardness; but direct them to it by what amuses their minds, so that you may be better able to discover with accuracy the peculiar bent of the genius in each.'

Plato

Tiger mums and dads

A recurring facet in the research is that successful adults have generally had some help from a significant person in their development. This often starts with the immediate family, a mother, father or grandparent. These 'tiger' mums and dads often are highly motivated by feelings of protection of their young and then astonishment and disgust at the unfairness in society of the way dyslexic people are treated. They are to be found in many countries in the world, spreading the word and trying to get improvements in education and the workplace.

Help with self-esteem

Their role with their children, though, in addition to selecting schools, and coaching them in reading and other homework, is most important in maintaining their child's self-esteem. Constantly reminding the child that they are valuable and loved; picking them up after knockdowns and re-motivating them to succeed. How to parent a dyslexic child is a book in itself, but I would urge parents picking up this book to look particularly at Chapter 2 on self-esteem.

Example of student mentoring schemes

Student mentoring schemes have become quite common. As an example, Eye to Eye in New York, U.S.A., who say their mission is 'to improve the life of every person with a learning disability. We fulfil our mission by supporting and growing a network of youth mentoring programmes run by and for those with learning differences, and by organising advocates to support the full inclusion of people with learning disabilities and A.D.H.D. in all aspects of society.' They pair up school children with dyslexia and related conditions with college and high school mentors so that the children can learn from those who have already travelled a similar journey.

Their evaluation of their scheme reports that 85 per cent of students felt better about themselves, and 87 per cent reported that their mentor helped them to think more positively about their future.

Fewer mentoring schemes for adults

It is less common to find schemes for adults, yet what dyslexics need is a close relationship with someone who has empathy with dyslexia. The research shows us that this can be quite transformational, especially for young adults getting started in the world.

The B.D.A. mentoring scheme for adults

In 2009, the British Dyslexia Association (B.D.A.), together with Dyslexia Scotland and the Cass Business School in London, embarked on a mentoring scheme for dyslexic adults. Here is their initial description:

> The B.D.A.'s mentoring scheme, in conjunction
> with Cass Business School, City University London,
> and Dyslexia Scotland was specifically created to
> be flexible. This emphasised two people getting
> together who share something in common – dyslexia.
> The scheme aimed to provide an opportunity for a
> mentor to share some of their coping strategies and
> above all instil confidence in the mentee. A principle

of recognising the positive attributes of being dyslexic formed our core approach to the scheme. The scheme was conceived to celebrate the positive side of dyslexia and who better to do this than the individuals who have travelled the same road and who can act as role models.

A key theme of the programme was its flexibility. The mentoring relationships were envisaged to be self-managed and directed so as to provide the opportunity for mentor and mentee to address issues most pertinent to them. Therefore, beyond the application and matching processes, mentors and mentees were responsible for arranging their own meetings.

How the scheme worked

Mentors were asked to provide 12 mentoring sessions over one year. The majority of these took place as personal meetings. However, as some mentor and mentee partnerships were spread across larger geographical areas and to accommodate work or other commitments, other means were also used to great effect; including the use of the internet-based system Skype.

Group mentoring sessions

In addition to individual mentoring, the programme also provided group mentoring sessions, which are one-off events comprising 5 or 6 individuals. These sessions were often hosted by one of the high-profile mentors. The evaluation contained some very interesting personal successes, but overall the striking outcome was the increase in self-confidence reported by all the mentees who participated in it.

It also led to interest in some large companies establishing their own schemes. British Telecom, which employed 90,000 employees in the U.K. at the time, showed interest; and Ernst & Young, a global financial services company, established a very active 'mentoring for dyslexics' scheme which continues today. Shell U.K. has also implemented a small-scale pilot scheme.

General principles for a dyslexia mentoring scheme

Since then, there have been more requests by companies and other organisations who want to set up their own mentoring schemes for dyslexic individuals. So, how do you do it? These mentoring schemes are not quite the same as a generic scheme that you might find in a management development programme. Here are the general principles for a dyslexia-related mentoring scheme:

- Focus on the experience or knowledge of dyslexia that the mentor has, rather than their level of seniority.

- Aim to improve the confidence of the mentee and to impart specific skills and knowledge that enable them to manage their lives better.

- Provide trust-building opportunities between mentors and mentees, as mentees may be divulging feelings and experiences that they have not told anyone else ever.

- Recruit and train a bank of mentors first. You will almost certainly find that you do not have enough mentors. You can seek mentors through newspapers, your and contacts' websites, press releases and via word of mouth. The training needs to cover: the aims of the scheme; how the scheme will operate (logistics); how to give support and advice to the mentee; how to deal with difficult situations; where to signpost mentees to when they need help beyond the scheme.

- Create a mentoring contract so everyone knows the expectations of the programme and each other.

- Use Skype or Hangouts or similar software to get around geographical issues.

- Make all your communications dyslexia-friendly.

So, that's all good from the perspective of setting up a dyslexia mentoring scheme, but what about if you are a dyslexic adult and are looking for a mentor? Where do you find a good one?

How do you find a mentor?

As with all relationships, you need to find someone you can get on with, and with whom there is that little bit of magic, some shared chemistry. So, you are basically on the lookout for someone to be your friend who also has the following traits:

- Experience of being dyslexic or knowing a lot about it and having empathy for dyslexic people.

- Trustworthy; you need to be able to tell them about things you have experienced which might make you feel very emotional.

- Resourceful; they need to know more than you do about managing your dyslexia or finding a route through life that works.

Ask family and friends for contacts

So, where will you find this special person? There are lots of places to start looking. First of all, look close to home. Is there someone already in your family or your immediate contacts that would be really good at being your mentor, except that up until now you hadn't really thought about this?

If not, then what about friends of friends, particularly of your dyslexic friends. Start asking around and let it be known that you are seeking a mentor, and you may find that someone is suggested to you.

Attend dyslexia group meetings

Attending local meetings of dyslexia charities or organisations can increase your exposure to new people. There are lots of online groups on social networking sites that you can also join and where you can search for someone meeting your criteria. For example, I belong to the Royal Society of Arts and did a search for 'Fellows' and 'Dyslexia' and immediately found 3 people I didn't know but could get in touch with. LinkedIn is another excellent and global place to look. You can also use Twitter to find individuals with topics in common. Start 'following' those who generate the sort of tweets you like and then you can send them a message and follow up from there. The world is literally your oyster for finding someone who can support your development.

Keep safe

Just a word on safety, though. Remember that these people are strangers to you at first. Don't agree to meet up with someone you don't know in an isolated spot. If you wouldn't go on a date with someone in these circumstances, then use the same judgement and use sensible safeguards about making connections.

Case study: Emad Rahim

Dr Emad Rahim is an award-winning author, entrepreneur and educator. He is a survivor of the genocide by the Khmer Rouge in Cambodia where he lost his father and older brother. Escaping the refugee camp in Thailand with his mother, baby sister and stepfather to the U.S.A. as a small boy, he grew up in poverty and violence in Brooklyn and Syracuse, New York, at the height of the crack epidemic. There were regular neighbourhood shootings and gang violence, and some of his schoolmates were killed.

He did not learn that he was dyslexic until he was studying, or rather struggling, at the local community college. At school he had been told he had a learning disability but did not receive any assistance. He was placed in E.S.L. (English as a Second Language) and special education classes in elementary school, placed in at-risk programmes in middle school, and enrolled in a vocational-focused programme called Occupational Learning Center in high school. Always a few years behind his peers in meeting appropriate academic comprehension levels, and barely graduating from his high school, his self-esteem took a big knock as a teenager.

At college his sociology (human service) lecturer recommended that he applied to the SUNY Empire State College, which is for adult students, and get tested for dyslexia through one of their mentors. The diagnosis was confirmed and Emad, aged 21, received guided mentorship and support. Learning in ways that suited his kinaesthetic needs resulted in him suddenly getting 'A' grades and he eventually earned his doctorate with honours. He went on to earn additional academic credentials, completing his post-doctoral studies at Tulane University, University of Maryland U.C. and Harvard University. He has gone on to found 2 enterprises, write 5 books and numerous articles, contribute to thinktanks, teach at universities and serve as a University Dean and M.B.A. Director. He is now Distinguished 'Entrepreneur in Residence' at Oklahoma State University, and is an Endowed Chair and Associate Professor at Bellevue University.

Dr Rahim's first enterprise was the Human Services Association of Central New York. This allowed him and his group of other business doctoral students to provide free workshops and training for social workers who needed to continue training but couldn't afford it. After 2 years, they started to get very successful and accrued additional funds from membership dues, training fees, donations and grants. After the success of his non-profit Association, Emad went on to co-found 2 new organisations and operate a successful business consultancy. He is currently an equity partner at IntelligentHQ.com and the Ztudium Group.

Dr Rahim is passionate about mentoring. He grew up without his birth father and with an abusive stepfather. He got into trouble at school. Fortunately, Mr Willie Dowdell was an administrator in his high school and took the young Emad under his wing. He ensured that Emad did not bunk off school, demanded good standards of behaviour, encouraged him and assisted him in applying to college. Dr Rahim advises new entrepreneurs and start-up teams at Syracuse University to surround themselves with good mentors and always look for opportunities to build their network. Learn as much as you can from others, he recommends, but he also recognises that a lot of people writing about leadership have never led. 'You can't talk about the frustration, the success, the sadness, the insecurity of leadership unless you've felt it yourself. You have to stay the course. I've had tons of setbacks. Then I reach out to others for different perspectives. I've had to lay people off and at the same time it was hurting inside. I've also been part of the celebrations when things went right. You have to be a life-long learner when it comes to leadership.'

Dr Rahim attributes much of his success to the help and support he has received from his friends, family and mentors in his life. He was able to overcome his learning disabilities and challenges with dyslexia with the help and guidance of people that cared and loved him. Mentors can be a powerful force in building a young person's self-esteem, pushing them to success and supporting them in making difficult decisions. Today, Emad helps mentor young people all around the United States through his work with the Good Life Youth Foundation, Dream Beyond Foundation and other service organisations. **Special note:** Emad's story was turned into a short documentary titled **Against the Odds** and incorporated into a Syracuse Stage Theater production titled

Tales from the Salt City written by celebrated playwright and Presidential National Medals of Arts recipient, Ping Chong. The documentary has been viewed by over 100,000 YouTube subscribers and was nominated for a visual storytelling award, and the play has since been published in **The Stone Canoe: A Journal of Arts and Ideas** (Syracuse University Press) and **CNY Magazine**. He was recognised as an Empact100 Honoree by the United Nations for his social entrepreneurship work, 40 Under Forty Business Leader by Whitman School of Business, and named Certified Manager of the Year from I.C.P.M. of James Madison University. He was the recipient of Bellevue University's Faculty of the Year Award in Innovation, Entrepreneurship Teaching Excellence Award from Oklahoma State University, and was a finalist for the John Robert Gregg Award in Business Education. In 2012 he participated in the Empact Summit, an invite-only entrepreneurship conference hosted at the White House and U.S. Chambers of Commerce in Washington D.C.

Key points from this chapter

★ Parents' engagement early on is important, especially in maintaining a child's self-confidence.

★ Later in life, a mentor can be transformational.

★ Rather than seniority, the mentor must be able to empathise with dyslexia and be able to share things such as coping strategies or signposts to support.

★ Mentoring schemes for dyslexic school children and students are quite widespread and effective at increasing self-esteem and recognition of individual strengths.

★ Mentoring schemes for adults are less common but can be set up using some simple recommendations.

★ The world is very well joined up now through social media and so finding your own dyslexia mentor is entirely possible.

Chapter 11

To Be Self-fulfilled You Have to Find a Balance

'Mens sana, in corpore sano' ('A healthy mind in a healthy body')

Plato

Life is busy and stress common

The individual strengths that many dyslexic adults self-report are like their magic powers. However, we also know that dyslexia, and other specific learning difficulties, make some things very hard to do. The more we live in a global economy with 24/7 communications, the more likely and dangerous it is that we are 'on alert' virtually all of the time. In addition, the tasks that are required when we are on alert are often the ones that we are not so comfortable about. All those emails and texts require reading. Sorting out our priorities amongst a large amount of correspondence and data requires excellent organisational skills. It is not surprising that people generally record higher levels of stress. The issue is, though, that for dyslexic adults, the stress is even greater.

Avoiding getting stressed

Then, on top of your existing life, I am recommending that to lead a successful life you might also want to increase your skills in the 10 areas covered in this book. It is essential, therefore, that we look at all of this within the context of a balanced and healthy life. It's no good if you are working so hard to be successful in one dimension that you suffer burn-out. So this final chapter is just about some basic good sense for your body and some key points about stress and the need to manage it. I have focused particularly on stress management because it is a particularly sensitive issue for dyslexic individuals. We depend on our coping strategies to thrive; and the problem is that if we get quite stressed, our coping strategies often fail. This is obviously a serious problem but one we can avoid with a bit of planning and a few tips.

Water and food

Our bodies are healthy when we give them the things they need to function. We wouldn't expect a car to run without fuel and the same is true of our bodies. Experts tell us that we need 2 litres of fluid a day to hydrate our bodies. This can be taken in various forms, such as liquid in our food, soups, decaffeinated drinks and water itself. We need to remember that tea and coffee contain caffeine, which is a stimulant, and they are also diuretics.

We are also advised to eat a varied diet with plenty of vegetables and to avoid too much salt or sugar.

Sleep

There are lots of studies into sleep at present showing how critical it is for helping our memories and keeping us healthy. Adults are said to need 7.5–8 hours per night to maintain healthy brain activity. It is also very important for managing stress. The key to good sleep is good sleep hygiene, which means winding down for about an hour before you go to bed, not having digital machines in the bedroom, and creating a routine so your body knows it's time to go to sleep.

Stress

Stress is the feeling of being under too much mental or emotional pressure. Pressure turns into stress when you feel unable to cope. People have different ways of reacting to stress, so a situation that feels stressful to one person may be motivating to someone else. As stated previously, though, the particular problem with stress for dyslexic individuals, as compared with other people, is that it can make their coping strategies collapse. This can then create a vicious circle where the individual becomes even more stressed as they cannot cope as well as usual.

Initial signs of stress

It is important to recognise the initial signs of stress so that you can take preventative action. Stress can affect how you feel, think, behave and how your body works. A common sign of stress is sleeping problems (finding it hard to get off to sleep initially or waking in the night and feeling anxious or with a busy brain). Other signs include difficulty focusing or concentrating, loss of appetite and sweating. Some individuals find that they are having racing thoughts or constantly go over things in their heads. You may suffer headaches, muscle pain or tension.

When stress becomes a danger

Some stress is good for us because it helps us learn how to deal with possible threats. The problem arises when the pressure is more than we can cope with or if it is continuous. Stress causes a surge in the stress hormones in our body which are designed to enable us to fight or take flight as a response to threat. Once the threat or pressure has passed, our stress hormone levels are supposed to return to normal. However, if we are constantly under stress, then these hormones will remain in the body and can lead to the symptoms of stress described above, or, worse, problems with our immune systems which can lead to serious illness.

Learning to manage stress

Undesirable stress is extremely common. So having recognised the signs of it, what can we do to manage it? Your first stage may be to keep a diary for a few days to see what is actually happening. From this you can spot triggers that might be causing you to feel under too much pressure. This first step is really important as it enables you to take control, rather than your situation controlling you.

Recent research has shown that people feel much better when they are in control, for example when affected by chronic illnesses, than if they feel controlled by their situation. So next, give yourself permission to take control and do something about it. Remember, you cannot achieve as much or help others if you are not in a good place yourself! This can be quite a challenge to do but it will be worth it and, from there, the rest of things are much easier.

Five things for rebalancing life

There are 5 things that are regularly recommended for rebalancing your life and managing your stress response. These are:

- **Connecting with others.** Humans are sociable animals; we need some social time with others. Connect with your family, your colleagues or people in your networks. You may find that you need to spend some time developing these relationships. Healthy relationships are 2-way – you give and, when you need it, they are there for you to receive their love and comfort.

- **Being active.** This doesn't mean you have to turn into an Olympic athlete, but we all need to move. Walking is particularly good at any age, but it's important that you find an activity that you like doing, otherwise you are likely to see this as a duty and that's not ideal for your mental wellbeing either.

- **Learning new skills.** We saw earlier that there is a link between learning and self-esteem. Learning to do something new gives you a sense of achievement and reinforces the idea that you are a competent person, which is very critical to self-confidence. This is also really important as we age, so that we keep our brains operating at their best.

- **Altruism, being kind and giving to someone else.** There is evidence that volunteers are more resilient to stress than others. It could be that seeing others' lives and problems gives perspective to our own. You can also be kind to yourself. In the research I did with dyslexic adults, I asked them what they would recommend to their younger selves and several individuals included being kind to themselves. Carve out a bit of time for yourself to just be, and let your body slip into a calm state.

- **Focusing on now.** You can find lots of material on the internet on mindfulness. This is about being 'in the moment'. You can learn to be more aware of the present moment, including your thoughts and feelings, your body and the world around you. It may take a bit of practice to learn how to focus on your breathing, where you are and how your body feels, but it does mean that you cannot actively worry while you are doing this. It will also slow your breathing and heart rate, which calms the stress hormones. This can positively change your perspective and build your resistance to pressures. If you find that you have a heightened emotional response to threats, so you get more upset, more angry than is proportionate to the event, you may find the following trick helpful to distract you immediately following whatever incident arouses you: do something that requires strong concentration and engages your rational brain. This could be a brain puzzle, something like Sudoku or a crossword if you like doing these, or play a card or board game such as patience or Mastermind. The distraction sometimes stops the hormones rising and gives you a chance to stand back from the event and gain perspective on it.

Key points from this chapter

★ It's crucial to lead a balanced life.

★ Stress is the enemy of our coping strategies.

★ We need to recognise the early signs of stress.

★ It's important to take back control of our lives and our reactions.

★ There are 5 widely recommended approaches to stress reduction.

Appendix A

Research Questionnaire into Issues for Adults with Dyslexia/Sp.L.D.

1. What do you put your key successes in life down to?

2. Have you had a formal diagnosis of dyslexia or related Sp.L.D.?

    Yes / No

    Or are you self-diagnosed as being dyslexic or with a related Sp.L.D.?

    Yes / No

3. On a scale of 1–10 (where 1 is low and 10 is high), how would you rate your self-esteem now?

4. Do you believe your dyslexia/Sp.L.D. has bestowed certain abilities on you?

   Yes / No

   If yes, what are they?

   Can you give some examples of what they have enabled you to do?

5. What are the major challenges that you face because of your dyslexia/Sp.L.D.?

6. What effect do you think these challenges have had on your life?

7. Is there a particular person who has had a significant impact on helping you to cope with your challenges and optimise your abilities?

   Yes / No

   If yes, was that person:

   a relative

   a dyslexia-trained coach

   a mentor

   someone within a network (e.g. Dyslexia Association)

   Other (please specify)

8. Have you ever disclosed your dyslexia/Sp.L.D. to an employer?

   Yes / No

   If yes, was the result positive or negative?

9. What would your advice be to a 20-year-old with dyslexia/Sp.L.D.?

Who filled in the questionnaire?

This questionnaire was answered by 15 individuals initially who were from a broad spectrum of backgrounds and locations. A further 17 individuals (2 of whom were not dyslexic but were knowledgeable about dyslexia) answered it. The latter group were attending the B.D.A.'s International Conference and so were either academics or tutors/teachers with a lot of knowledge about dyslexia. There were some interesting differences between some of the answers from the 2 groups.

It was a strength of the study that answers could be given free format but, of course, that makes analysing the results more difficult. So it was necessary to accept some close synonyms. For example, in the first question lots of people did say 'determination' but others said 'persistence' and these are both grouped under determination. The findings were as follows.

Causes of key successes

	Group 1	Group 2
Determination	8	10
Motivated by helping others	3	5
Empathetic	6	4
Wit	4	0
Hard work	0	3
Effective education	0	3
Intelligence or particular ability	0	4
Supportive family	4	2

Comment

In analysing the 2 groups' responses, we need to be aware that this is asking people to self-report and so, for example, I found that the second group of academics ascribed their success to a mixture of determination and hard work in a subject they were already good at. They also reported that their intelligence was a key element of their success and that this had nothing to do with their dyslexia. It was apparent, though, that having an effective education and particularly sympathetic teachers had had a significant effect on this group compared with the first group. Interestingly, the controls also put down 'determination' and 'hard work' as their primary reasons for success.

Diagnoses of dyslexia

Group 1	Group 2
Diagnosed 12 Self-diagnosed 2	Diagnosed 11 Self-diagnosed 4

Levels of self-esteem

Group 1	Group 2
Range 5–10 Mode 8	Range 6–9 This group also reported variability according to recent experience

Abilities perceived to be from dyslexia

	Group 1	Group 2
Yes	7	9
No	2	3
Seeing big picture	7	7
Atypical problem solving	5	5
Coping strategies	1	0
Spatial awareness	0	0
Data patterns	2	1
Determination	5	1
Empathy	3	4
Inspiring others	3	1

Comment

I found it very interesting that the second group didn't attribute their successes so much to strengths arising out of dyslexia. However, they did recognise that they had these strengths of seeing the big picture, atypical problem solving and empathy to much the same degree as the first group which did ascribe their success to the special strengths endowed by dyslexia.

Major challenges faced as a result of dyslexia

	Group 1	Group 2
Literacy	12	8
Memory particularly affecting organisation	5	10
Background distractions	4	1
Getting lost	3	0
Learning is difficult	2	0

Effect of the challenges on life

	Group 1	Group 2
Considerable difficulties	Many	0
Under-achievement	5	2
Relationship issues (personal and professional)	9	1
Lack of self-belief	3	0
Stress and health issues	6	3

Support

	Group 1	Group 2
No one	3	3
Mentor	3	2
Dyslexia coach	6	3
Network member	3	3
Relative or spouse	4	8
Sympathetic teacher	0	3
Sympathetic boss	0	2

Disclosure

	Group 1	Group 2
No	3	4
Yes	9	11
Positive experience	5	11
Negative experience	4	0

What would you recommend to a young person?

	Group 1	Group 2
Learn coping strategies	9	9
Take or ask for help	3	4
Recognise you are different but not less worthy	4	2
Get a diagnosis early	3	2
Don't worry, it will all work out	4	4
Look for things you are good at	0	6
Develop a positive mindset	0	5

Appendix B

Notes on Dyslexia and Related Conditions

Roughly 15 per cent of the global population have Specific Learning Difficulties (Sp.L.D.s), including dyslexia, which is the most well-known of these. Sp.L.D.s are due to a particular genetic difference which affects the development of the brain; though we also know that environment plays its part in increasing the risk, or bestowing compensations, as the individual's brain develops. Post-mortem studies have shown us that the cells in the cerebellum are differently arrayed in those with a Sp.L.D. We also know from brain imaging scanning that activities one would expect to be carried out in certain areas of the brain are located differently in the brains of those with this condition.

The underlying genetic differences in the brain result in at least 8 diagnosable conditions, though these all overlap. Some of them you have probably heard of but may not realise that they are linked to each other.

These related conditions are all described briefly below. The brains of affected individuals will mean that they are faced with certain difficulties in life but the condition may also confer some unique strengths. The 8 co-occurring conditions can all be considered to be about taking in information and manipulating it, and there is generally a problem with working memory.

Dyslexia

People with this condition have a problem with identifying small differences in sounds or symbols and they generally also have a problem with working memory. The consequence of difficulties identifying the difference between certain close sounds, such as the vowels 'e' and 'i', or the soft consonants 'm' and 'f', is that it makes learning to read and spell very much more difficult. In addition, many individuals with dyslexia find that they have great difficulty learning the meaning of symbols, which affects their ability to learn the alphabet and to read easily.

Whilst what we hear about dyslexia is that it is a problem with learning to read and spell, in fact this is a consequence of the condition. In adults, challenges arise more from the other issues it confers on self-organisation and memory. These affect all of life's activities, from managing one's time to running a home. However, there are good coping strategies that we know about. When people learn about their dyslexia and how it particularly affects them, and start to use their coping strategies, it allows their strengths to become more obvious.

Dyscalculia

This is the name given to the condition where individuals have a problem with number recognition and arithmetic calculations. They may feel they are not 'hard-wired' for number concepts. Again, we rely on symbol recognition for arithmetic and so if this is impaired then problems can arise. That said, there is often no issue for the individuals when it comes to higher maths, which is based on problem solving, and can be a unique strength for those with Sp.L.D.s.

A.D.H.D. and A.D.D.

These are the 2 attention deficit disorders, with or without hyperactivity. The genetic inheritance in this case leads to an immaturity in the frontal lobes of the brain. This is where the 'brakes on our behaviour' are located. Consequently, the individual affected by this will find it much more difficult to focus on a particular activity and to prioritise their actions, and may appear to be very impulsive. Where they are hyperactive, it is because they are trying to respond to all the stimuli present. Those with A.D.D. (i.e. without hyperactivity) cope by zoning out from the stimuli around them, and so may seem to daydream.

Asperger's Syndrome

Those with this condition have difficulty recognising facial expressions and body language, and dealing with non-transparent language such as metaphors. It is not the same as autism, where the individual is likely to be non-communicative. This milder form of inability linked to communication issues is present in about 3 per cent of the population and the genetic background is not the same as that for individuals with autism (which is present in 1:3000 of the population).

Dyspraxia, D.C.D.

This is the name we give to difficulty with gross motor coordination. The individual may appear clumsy and, in addition, they may have problems with coordinating concepts and sequencing ideas and priorities. It is essentially about taking in information from our larger muscles and responding to it, and also the coordination of information within the cognitive processes of the brain. More commonly now it is known as Developmental Coordination Disorder (D.C.D.).

Dysgraphia

This is the name given to issues of coordination and manipulation of information for fine motor control. It can result in illegible handwriting and poor dexterity.

Specific Speech and Language Impairment

We know that speech problems in young children are the best indicator that they may suffer from dyslexic difficulties in later life. However, therapy can assist the child to develop better speech although some problems may persist into adulthood. These particularly tend to relate to storage of vocabulary and word retrieval. The impact of this can be a difficulty in expressing oneself adequately and being able to retrieve the right word at will.

Visual distraction

About half the individuals with a Sp.L.D. also suffer from visual stress. This is an extreme hypersensitivity to glare. It means that the person perceives print with a distortion. This can be very severe and mean that after just a few minutes of studying a document with black print on white, their eyes may stream and they cannot continue reading. Fortunately, it is generally very easily coped with by changing the colour of the paper to a pastel shade or wearing coloured-lensed glasses or changing the colour of the computer screen. (This is also suffered by others who may have migraines or be epileptic.) The condition is known by various names, including Irlen Syndrome or Meares-Irlen Syndrome, as well as visual stress or distraction.

Working memory difficulties

It is rare to find someone with one of the conditions listed above that does not have some difficulties with working memory. We have a number of different memory systems, such as muscle memory where we are able to learn, retain and retrieve memories about movement such as golf swing or a tennis serve. Working memory is a dynamic part of our memory system which is used to hold and manipulate information in real time. Often people describe their working memory as a shelf, and many of those with dyslexia say their shelf can only hold 3 things before it crashes. As we use our working memory for most things in life, such as learning and performing activities, it is clear that a deficit in this area creates a need for good coping strategies to get around any difficulties.

What to do if you think you may be dyslexic or have one of the other Sp.L.D.s

If you wish to, you can find out more by undertaking a screening test and potentially have a full diagnostic assessment. You can find screening tests on most of the dyslexia charity websites (it is advisable to search on the charity websites as their resources will have been examined for validity). A screening test will give you a response as to your likelihood of having dyslexia, but it is not foolproof. The only way you will really know if you have a Sp.L.D. is by going through a full diagnostic assessment. These assessments are carried out by psychologists in many countries but also in the U.K. by specialist dyslexia teachers who hold a level 7 qualification.

The assessment interview usually takes 3 hours and a range of tests will be used to identify various aspects such as your general ability level, your underlying cognitive abilities (such as working memory scores) and attainments in literacy and numeracy. The assessor will also be observing your approach to these tasks to see if they can recommend further resources or helpful things for you. As this is such a detailed task and can only be undertaken by individuals who have done very long and extensive training, diagnostic assessments are quite expensive (in the order of £500 in the U.K., or $500 in the U.S.A.). However, the final report will include recommendations for coping strategies, which most people find very helpful.

However, not everyone wants to be 'labelled', and that is a matter of personal taste. There is research that shows that individuals who are diagnosed have a better understanding and self-concept after the initial feelings post-diagnosis have subsided.

Resources

In any event, you will find very helpful and often free resources on the websites of the main dyslexia and Sp.L.D. charities. So I would refer you to:

The British Dyslexia Association:
www.bdadyslexia.org.uk

The Dyslexia Foundation:
www.dyslexiafoundation.co.uk

Dyslexia Action: www.dyslexiaaction.org.uk

Dyslexia Scotland: www.dyslexiascotland.org.uk

Dyslexia Ireland: www.dyslexia.ie

European Dyslexia Association: www.eda-info.eu

In the U.S.A., the International Dyslexia Association: www.dyslexiaida.org

In Brazil, the Instituto A.B.C.D. (which has a partnership with the B.D.A.): www.institutoabcd.org.br

Bibliography

Creative Dyslexic Adults, Margaret Rooke, 2015. London: Jessica Kingsley Publishers.

Entering Tiger Country: How Ideas are Shaped in Organizations, Jean Lammiman and Michel Syrett, 2000. Horsham: Roffey Park Institute.

Grit: The Power of Passion and Perseverance, Angela Duckworth, 2016. London: Vermillion Penguin.

The Adult Dyslexic: Interventions and Outcomes, David McLoughlin, Carol Leather and Patricia Stringer, 2002. London: Whurr.

The Adult Dyslexic: Interventions and Outcomes – An Evidence-based Approach (Second edition). David McLoughlin and Carol Leather, 2013. London: B.P.S. Blackwell.

The Art of Problem Solving, Russell L. Ackoff, 1978. New York: Wiley.

'45 highly successful dyslexic adults and 25 moderately successful dyslexic adults,' Paul Gerber, 2016. B.D.A. International Conference.

'Dyslexia and the life course,' Michael A. McNully, 2003. *Journal of Learning Disabilities 36*, 4, 363–381.

'Factors influencing work participation in adults with dyslexia,' Joost De Beer *et al.*, 2014. *BMC Public Health 14*, 77.

'Identifying alterable patterns in employment success for highly successful adults with learning disabilities,' Paul Gerber, 1992. *Journal of Learning Disabilities 25*, 8, 475–487.

'Procrastination rates among adults with and without ADHD: a pilot study,' Joseph R. Ferrari and Sarah E. Sanders, 2006. *Counselling and Clinical Psychology 3*, 2–9.

'Psychological resources of adults with developmental dyslexia,' Marta Lockiewicz, Katarzyna M. Bogdanowicz and Marty Bogdanowicz, 2014. *Journal of Learning Disabilities 47*, 6, 543–555.

'Successful careers: the secrets of adults with dyslexia,' Rosalie P. Fink, 2002. *USA Career Planning and Adult Development Journal 18*, 1, 118–135.

'The prevalence of dyslexia among art students,' Ulrika Wolff and Ingvar Lundberg, 2002. *Dyslexia 8*, 1, 34–42.

'What the research tells us about team creativity and innovation,' Roger Schwarz, 2015. *Harvard Business Review, 15 December*. Available at https://hbr.org/2015/12/what-the-research-tells-us-about-team-creativity-and-innovation, accessed on 24 October 2016.

Publications by the British Dyslexia Association, which include a Handbook each year containing articles on current thinking and research: *Dyslexia and Multilingualism; Dyslexia at Work* (written by Margaret Malpas); *Coping Strategies for Adults; Dyslexia, Music and the Performing Arts*. All available from http://www.bdastore.org.uk.

Also substantial work on adults by Blace Navalany and Lena Williams Carawan from East Carolina University, U.S.A. Most recently presented at the B.D.A. International Conference, 2016.